SELECTED LIST OF PUBLICATIONS
DIVISION OF RESEARCH

more complete list of publications appears at the end of this volume.

Alternative Commercial

Their Effect on the
Economy

Alternative Commerical Policies —

Their Effect on the American Economy

MORDECHAI E. KREININ

Professor of Economics
Graduate School of Business Administration
Michigan State University

1967
MSU INTERNATIONAL BUSINESS
AND ECONOMIC STUDIES
Institute for International Business
and Economic Development Studies
Division of Research
Graduate School of Business Administration
Michigan State University
East Lansing, Michigan

*To the memory of
my mother, Joheved*

Preface

This monograph is an expanded version of my contribution to the study of alternative trade arrangements in the Atlantic Community, sponsored by the Council on Foreign Relations in New York, under the general editorship of Professor Bela Balassa.[1] Parts of the manuscript were published in professional journals. But the estimates have since been changed somewhat because of refinements and improvements in the estimation procedures.

The bulk of this volume is concerned with quantitative estimates of the effects of various commercial policies on the external position and on the domestic economy of the United States. Although various trade arrangements are considered in connection with the U. S. balance of trade (Part II), the effect of an Atlantic Free Trade Area (AFTA) is the main focus of attention in Parts III and IV. Of the policies examined here an AFTA constitutes the most radical departure from present trade arrangements, and it would be virtually impossible to distinguish its effect on the U. S. capital account and on the domestic economy from those of more moderate proposals.

In constructing the quantitative estimates, assumptions had to made concerning tariffs, import demand and export supply elasticities, marginal propensities, and other variables. These assumptions are always explicitly stated, supported by whatever empirical evidence and a priori reasoning is available. In each case, I selected the assumption which appeared most reasonable to me. But in some instances I present comparative estimates based on alternative assumptions, in order to demonstrate the sensitivity of the results to the assumptions. The reader who so chooses, may select another set of assumptions, which he considers more realistic, and employ the same technique to construct alternative estimates.

vii

I wish to express my gratitude to the Council on Foreign Relations for sponsoring the original study and for continuous interest in the project, to Professor Bela Balassa for helpful comments and suggestions on earlier drafts, and to Mr. Tracy Murray for able computational assistance. I am also grateful to the *Economic Journal*, the *Review of Economics and Statistics*, the *American Economic Review*, the *Southern Economic Journal, Current Economic Comment*, and *Economia Internazionale* for permission to reproduce material from my articles published in these journals.

Mordechai E. Kreinin
June, 1967
East Lansing, Michigan

---

[1]The study, *Studies in Trade Liberalization,* is to be published by the Johns Hopkins University Press.

Contents

List of Tables

Table		*Page*
14	Employment Effects of Trade Liberalization (SIC Industries)	132
15	Major SITC Industries Affected by AFTA	135
16	SIC Export Industries Expected to Benefit from AFTA	138
17	SIC Import-Competing Industries Expected to be Injured by AFTA	139

Chapter 1
Foreign Trade in the American Economy

Despite the fact that the United States is a leading exporter of manufactured commodities,[4] it is often described as a "closed economy." The term refers to the fact that, quantitatively, foreign trade occupies a relatively small proportion of total economic activity. Because of its economic size and the diversity of its resources, the American economy can satisfy consumer wants and national needs with a minimum of reliance on foreign trade. This is in contrast with other industrial economies[5] in which foreign trade plays a significant, if not a dominant, role. The ratio of foreign trade to the production of traded commodities is much smaller in the United States than in most other industrial countries.

To be sure, quantitative measures never tell the entire story. They must be modified by qualitative considerations. To say that

---

[4] In 1963, United States Gross National Product exceeded that of all other industrial countries combined. Its exports of manufactured commodities were one-fifth of the total for all the industrial nations, topped only slightly by the share of Germany. Note that most trade negotiations are concerned with manufactures, and tariff rates on primary commodities are quite low. Consequently, it is the industrial component of trade which determines a country's bargaining position.

[5] It is also in sharp contrast to underdeveloped countries, where foreign trade is not only of crucial quantitative importance, but is also said to be the main generator of fluctuations in the domestic economy. (See Henry C. Wallich, "Underdeveloped Countries and the International Monetary Mechanism," in *Money, Trade, and Economic Growth*, essays in honor of J. H. Williams, New York: Macmillan Co., 1951, pp. 15-32.)

in 1963, U. S. merchandise imports ($17 billion) amounted to less than 3 percent of Gross National Product ($585 billions) is to understate the importance of these imports in several respects. American imports contain important primary commodities which cannot be produced domestically, but which are crucial for numerous productive processes. Their absence would have curtailed considerably domestic production, lowered consumer satisfaction, and interfered with our ability to meet national goals. Over 70 percent of U. S. agricultural imports are of "complementary commodities," namely commodities, such as tropical products, which cannot be grown in the United States. And while most manufacturing imports compete directly with domestically produced substitutes, foreign trade widens consumer choice through diversification of available products, and expands the producer's horizons in marketing his products and investing his capital. Opening the economy to the fresh winds of foreign competition also adds to its viability by spurring technological progress and other advances.[6] Moreover, the external payments position of the country, of which merchandise trade is the major component, influences aggregate output and income indirectly, through its effect on government fiscal and monetary policies. And finally, American imports constitute an important source of foreign exchange earnings for many underdeveloped countries, the stability of which is vital to the United States. It would therefore be misleading to suggest that the elimination or contraction of foreign trade would work no hardship on the American economy.

However, even the quantitative importance of foreign trade cannot be judged solely by using broad aggregative measures because its impact is not evenly spread over all sectors of the economy. A substantial portion of GNP is made up of such items as construction activities and various services, many of which never enter international trade, and will not be directly affected by changes in trade policies. Most of the direct effects would be concentrated in the commodity producing sectors. Table 1 relates exports and imports to domestic production and consumption in three main sectors[7] of the economy. Exports appear to be most important in agriculture, while imports

---

[6]For a detailed discussion of these and other points, see U. S. Department of Commerce, "The Role of Foreign Trade in the United States Economy" in *Foreign Trade Policy,* Compendium of Papers on United States Foreign Trade Policy, Subcommittee on Foreign Trade Policy, Committee on Ways and Means, United States Congress, Washington, 1958, pp. 15-22.

are most significant among mineral commodities. Of these three sectors, the specific concern of this study is with manufacturing, because any Atlantic trade arrangement is likely to abolish or reduce trade restrictions on manufactured commodities but make some special provisions for other products.

Table 1

Relation of Foreign Trade to Domestic Production and Consumption

Sector	Domestic Production ($ Billions)	Export As Percent of Production	Imports As Percent of Apparent Consumption[a]
Agriculture (1960)	30.1	11.3	7.4
Minerals (1960)	17.9	3.3	10.1
Manufacturing (1962)	399.3	4.3	2.7

a. Production plus imports minus exports.

SOURCES: U. S. Department of Agriculture, *Census of Agriculture, 1959,* 1960 Sample; U. S. Department of the Interior, *Minerals Yearbook,* Vol. III, 1960; Bureau of the Census, *Annual Survey of Manufacturing,* 1962; Bureau of the Census, *U. S. Commodity Exports and Imports as Related to Output,* 1960 and 1959, Washington, D. C., 1962.

In 1962, the manufacturing sector, as defined by the U. S. Census Bureau (divisions 20-39 in the Standard Industrial Classification), constituted somewhat less than one-third of GNP, with value added of $179.3 billion. Total shipments approximated $400 billion, while exports and imports amounted to $17 and $10.7 billion, respectively. In relation to total merchandise trade, finished manufactures formed 79 percent of all exports and 66 percent of all imports. Finally, foreign trade comprised a small proportion of shipments in all the twenty SIC industry divisions, and exports exceeded 10 percent of production in the case of nonelectrical machinery only (Table 2).

But even these figures are too aggregative. Foreign trade among industrial nations is extremely specialized, and any one of the twenty SIC divisions may contain large variations which are not reflected in the industry averages. Published data on the relationship between trade and domestic output permits disaggregation to the four-digit SIC level. Of the 271 SIC industries for which comparable exports and production figures are available, 221 industries have an export-output ratio below 10 percent.[8] Only fifty industries have a ratio

[7]Forestry and Fisheries are excluded.

[8]Bureau of the Census, *U. S. Commodity Exports and Imports as Related to Output,* 1962 and 1961, Washington, 1964, pp. 2 and 4.

Table 2

U. S. Exports and Imports as Related to the Value of Domestic Production and Consumption, 1962

SIC Code	Industry	Value of Shipments ($ Billions)	Exports As Percentage of Value of Production	Import as Percentage of Apparent Consumption[a]
20	Food and Kindred Products	66.9	2.5	2.9
21	Tobacco Manufactures	4.5	2.6	0.0
22	Textile Mill Products	15.1	2.0	4.6
23	Apparel and Related Products	16.1	0.9	2.3
24	Lumber and Wood Products	8.4	2.3	6.8
25	Furniture and Fixtures	5.5	0.5	0.5
26	Paper and Allied Products	15.7	2.9	6.8
27	Printing and Publishing Products	15.6	1.0	0.4
28	Chemicals and Allied Products	29.4	7.5	1.7
29	Petroleum and Coal Products	17.2	2.6	4.3
30	Rubber and Plastic Products, n.e.c.	8.5	2.0	1.4
31	Leather and Leather Products	4.3	1.2	4.3
32	Stone, Clay, and Glass Products	11.5	1.9	2.2
33	Primary Metal Products	34.0	2.6	4.1
34	Fabricated Metal Products, n.e.c.	22.3	2.7	0.9
35	Machinery, Except Electrical	28.4	13.0	2.0
36	Electrical Machinery	27.6	4.6	1.8
37	Transportation Equipment	51.3	5.5	1.4
38	Instruments and Related Products	6.6	8.0	3.5
39	Miscellaneous Manufactured Products	10.4	1.7	3.9
	All Manufactures	399.3	4.3	2.7

SOURCES: Value of Shipments: U. S. Bureau of the Census, *Annual Survey of Manufactures, 1962.* Foreign trade: U. S. Bureau of the Census, *U. S. Commodity Exports and Imports as Related to Output 1962 and 1961.* Washington, 1964.

exceeding this level, and their total exports amounted to $7.1 billion. Thus, 18 percent of the industries account for 45 percent of total manufacturing exports. On the imports side, 196 out of the 233 comparable industries have an import-supply ratio of less than 10 percent. The remaining 37 industries, which constitute 16 percent of the total number, account for 39 percent of total imports. The following lists identify eighteen manufactured commodity groups whose exports in 1960 exceeded 10 percent of output and which were valued at more than $100 million, and fourteen manufactured groups whose 1961 imports were more than 10 percent of new supply (domestic output plus imports), with a value of over $50 million.[9]

---

[9]See, Committee on Economic Development, *Trade Negotiations For A Better Free World Economy,* Washington, 1964, pp. 38, 39.

Leading Exports: condensed and evaporated milk; flour and meal; milled rice; grease and inedible tallow; synthetic rubber; internal combustion engines; farm machinery; construction and mining machinery; metal-cutting machine tools; oil field machinery; metal-forming machine tools; textile machinery; pumps and compressors; computing and related machines; aircraft and engines; aircraft parts, etc.; railroad, streetcar, etc.; photographic equipment.

Leading Imports: raw cane sugar; wine and brandy; distilled liquor except brandy; vegetable oil mill products; scouring and combing mill products; textile goods, n.e.c.; sawmill products; pulp mill products; paper mill products; rubber footwear; refined lead; nonferrous smelter; watches and clocks; lapidary work.

There is of course no certainty that the industries most severely influenced by changes in commercial policies would be those which are now heavily engaged in foreign trade. On the import side, there are industries in which the ratio of imports to new supplies is low *because* of tariff protection and which would be affected by a drastic reduction in import duties. Likewise, exports depend to some extent on the level of protection in foreign countries, and the same argument applies there, although with less cogency. Needless to say, the industries affected by trade liberalization will further depend on the structure of comparative advantage among the industrial countries.

However, the above figures do point to two important conclusions. Most American manufacturing industries are relatively independent of foreign trade, and are likely to remain so even if their volume of trade were doubled. Secondly, there are a few industries in which foreign trade plays an important role, and which may suffer or enjoy a concentrated impact in the event of drastic trade liberalization. That impact may also be concentrated in certain geographical regions.

Because of the minor position occupied by foreign trade in the aggregate national economy, it is fitting that special attention be paid to the effect of policy changes on the balance of payments. For while changes in the volume of industrial trade are likely to constitute a small percentage of domestic production, they would form a significant portion of total trade and payments, and could sway the "basic balance"[10] in either direction. Since fiscal and (primarily) monetary policies are governed to some extent by the external payments position of the country, the domestic economy would bear some of the consequences of commercial policy measures through the external payments mechanism.

---

[10]The "basic balance" is one of the three commonly used concepts for measuring the surplus or deficit in the balance of payments. It includes "above the line" the current account items (i.e. trade in goods and services), unilateral transfers, and long-term capital movements. On the other hand, short term capital flows as well as gold movements, are treated as the balancing items and are placed "below the line."

Chapter 2

U. S. Commercial Policy—
Historical Perspective

A. POLITICAL CONSIDERATIONS IN U. S. COMMERCIAL POLICY

Given the small share of foreign trade in the American economy
and the emergence of the United States as the leading Western country,
it may not be surprising that political (or military) rather than economic considerations governed our decisions in the field of commercial policy during much of the postwar era.[11] This point can be
abundantly illustrated by American attitudes toward European affairs.
In the immediate postwar years, the United States supported the
liberalization of intra-European trade and payments, carried out by
the OEEC[12] and the EPU[13] respectively, even though both arrangements discriminated against American exports to western Europe.
Although the acute dollar shortage of that period provided an economic rationale for such a policy, the real basis for it was a desire
to achieve political stability and military viability on the continent.
Likewise, the United States lent its support to the creation of the
European Coal and Steel Community under the Schuman plan, and
subsequently backed the establishment of the European Economic
Community (EEC) and the European Atomic Energy Community.[14]

---

[11]For a complete discussion of this point see Bela Balassa, *Trade Liberalization
in Industrial Countries: Objectives and Alternatives,* Council on Foreign Relations,
N.Y., Chap. 2.

[12]Organization for European Economic Cooperation.

[13]European Payments Union.

The likelihood that the EEC would affect American exports to the Six unfavorably, primarily the sales of agricultural products, was evidently given little weight in the formulation of American policy, as was the possible adverse effect of the newly created union on the relative bargaining power of the United States in international economic negotiations. The overriding consideration was the presumed political advantage to be drawn from a strong Europe in cold war politics and other matters. It goes without saying that the United States expected to remain the unchallenged leader of a stronger Western alliance, and hoped that the community would be "outward looking" in its commercial policies.

American advocacy of United Kingdom entry into the EEC was motivated by the desire to strengthen the latter organization and to enhance U. S. influence on its policies.[15] But this country opposed the creation of an all European Free Trade Area, and assumed a rather lukewarm attitude toward EFTA presumably because these organizations were regarded by the Administration as mere trade associations, which would not contribute significantly to the political strength of Europe. In a similar vein, the American opposition to the entry of the "neutral" countries (Sweden, Austria, and Switzerland) to the EEC can be explained by the fear of diluting the political content of the community.

The exclusive emphasis on political considerations[16] has changed somewhat in the 1960's, and transformed into what might be called a political-economic mix. In large measure the change can be traced to the emergence of the EEC as a strong bargaining unit in GATT negotiations and as a market whose policy can significantly affect U. S. exports. The fact that the United States, for the first time in postwar history, is facing an economic power of almost equal strength across the bargaining table, coupled with the impending adverse repercussions of EEC discrimination on American exports, has led to the aforementioned shift. The changes found their most explicit expression in the Trade Expansion Act of 1962. But it cannot be overemphasized that the increasing political strength of the EEC,

---

[14]Today, the United States channels all its assistance to the Six in matters of atomic energy through Euratom. See *The New York Times,* Nov. 20, 1966, p. 4.

[15]See the *Wall Street Journal,* January 24, 1967, p. 14.

[16]The United States is not at all unique in this respect. Many countries regard foreign economic policies as part of foreign policy, and assign their foreign minister all responsibilities in foreign trade matters.

with the attendant erosion of the American leadership position in Europe, has also contributed to the transformation of U. S. policies.

B. The Reciprocal Trade Agreements Legislation

The illustrations given in the last section relate primarily to behind the scene diplomatic activity, and of necessity, are conjectural in nature. But similar conclusions concerning the motives underlying American commercial policy can be drawn from legislative history in trade matters. The cornerstone of American commercial policy in the past thirty years has been the Trade Agreements Act, initiated in 1934 and continued through periodic extensions throughout the postwar years. American participation in GATT's tariff negotiations is implicitly sanctioned by this legislation, as is the extent of duty reductions permissible at any one "Round" of bargaining. The provisions of the Act, as well as their administration, provide the most explicit clues to the motives of U. S. commercial policies.

Two main lines of thought thread through the successive extensions of the reciprocal trade legislation, although their relative importance varied from one extension to another. On the one hand, the legislation permitted continual, though limited, tariff reductions on U. S. imports. During the postwar years, such reductions have been negotiated within the multilateral framework of GATT, subject to the unconditional most-favored-nation principal. Bargaining has proceeded on a product-by-product basis. And, like other nations, the United States has bargained only with major suppliers of each commodity, and resorted to redefinition of products, in order to avoid offering free concessions to third countries. On the other hand, most extensions of the law embodied a "no injury" philosophy; that is, trade liberalization was to be accomplished with a minimum of injury to domestic industry. This philosophy found expression in the escape clause, peril point, and national security provisions of the Act.[17]

To the economist, the no injury approach is clearly inconsistent with the general spirit of the reciprocal trade legislation. He regards tariff reduction first and foremost as a means to improve economic efficiency through increased international specialization. A larger volume of trade is expected to drive domestic resources away from

---

[17]In the diplomatic sphere, the no injury philosophy was also promoted by inducing Japan to restrict "voluntarily" the exports of cotton-textiles, and other products to the United States.

relatively inefficient import-competing industries, into industries in which we have competitive advantage. A similar process would take place abroad with the obvious result of increased efficiency all around. The escape clause is essentially a mechanism for preventing such a shift of resources. By protecting industries from import competition it perpetuates allocative inefficiency, and is therefore considered to be in direct conflict with what the Act set out to accomplish. On the one hand, we reduce tariffs and admit larger imports; but the instant such imports begin to have the salutary effect of driving resources out of inefficient uses, we call off the medicine.

This view of the main purpose of the tariff reduction program is by no means universal. It is certainly not shared by many legislators and public officials. In these circles the program was regarded primarily as a means of expanding American exports and of strengthening the Western Alliance.

The Trade Agreements Act was originally proposed by the Roosevelt Administration in 1934 as an anti-depression measure, designed to open up new export markets for American products. The offer of tariff concessions on a reciprocal basis was not an end in itself. Rather, it was meant to constitute an inducement to foreign countries to open their markets to American products. This view, while still widely held, has been superceded in the postwar period by a politically oriented objective. The program came to be commonly regarded as a means of strengthening the economies of friendly nations through opening the American market to some of their products, as symbolized by the slogan, "Trade not aid." The postwar dollar shortage contributed considerably to the importance of this objective. Most proponents of the Trade Agreements Program—be they administration officials or representatives of other public bodies and private interests —stressed these two purposes when testifying before congressional committees in support of extending the Act. The economic end of attaining higher efficiency is usually given some lip service, but is not held in high regard.

To these officials, there exists no real inconsistency between an extensive tariff reduction program on the one hand and the prevention of injury to domestic interests on the other. If U. S. aims are the opening of new export markets and the cementing of the Western Alliance—why not attain them at the least cost in terms of displacement of domestic production?

THE 1958 EXTENSION

This indeed was the major trend in the reciprocal trade leg-islation since the Randall Report of 1954. The Randall Commission, which was set up by the Eisenhower Administration to study the goals of U. S. foreign economic policies, recommended the continua-tion of the Trade Agreements Program with appropriate safeguards to domestic industry. The subsequent extensions of the Act during the 1950's—a three-year extension in 1955 and a four-year[18] one in 1958—contained liberal provisions for tariff reduction (averaging 5 percent per year). The latter legislation, for example, authorized the President to offer concessions of up to 20 percent of the July 1, 1958 tariff rates, to be spread evenly over a four-year period.[19] Alternatively, the President was permitted to cut tariff rates by two percentage points, or to reduce to fifty percent ad valorem all rates in excess of that level. These two alternatives are significant in cases where the 1958 rates were below ten percent or above 62.5 percent, respectively.[20]

At the same time, however, Congress strengthened considerably

---

[18]All eleven extensions granted earlier ranged from one to three years in length.

[19]Even this provision fell short of the Administration's request for a five-year extension with tariff cutting authority of 25 percent (or, alternately, three per-centage points), despite the rather compelling reasons advanced on its behalf. First, it was deemed necessary to assure foreign nations of America's intention to follow an enduring policy of trade liberalization in order to inspire confidence and promote long-run trade commitments. Secondly, the requested five-year extension would have corresponded timewise to the integration schedule of the European Common Market. The first step in establishing the common external tariff by the Six was planned for 1963. Similarly, a 25 percent tariff cutting au-thority would have been roughly compatible with the plan to lower intra-com-mon market tariff rates by 30 percent by 1963. This authority, coupled with a requested carry-over provision (namely, permission to put into effect any time after the five-year period tariff cuts negotiated during that period), would have made possible fruitful negotiations with the Common Market for mutual tariff concessions within the framework of the GATT. In addition to minimizing dis-crimination against American exports, such negotiations would have served to keep the Common Market tariff low in the interest of world trade. This could be more easily accomplished before producers in the Six become accustomed to high tariffs.

[20]Passage of the Bill, on August 20, 1958, followed extensive hearings before the House Ways and Means Committee (covering 2935 pages) and the Senate Finance Committee (covering 1518 pages). See *Renewal of Trade Agreements Act*, Hearings before the Committee on Ways and Means, Eighty-fifth Congress, Second Session; and *Trade Agreements Act Extension*, Hearings before the Com-mittee on Finance, Eighty-fifth Congress, Second Session.

the protection to domestic interests against import competition. Three avenues of protection were open to domestic industries. First, under the peril point provision the United States Tariff Commission was required to investigate and determine, *prior* to any negotiations, the level below which the tariff rate on each product could not be lowered without causing serious injury to a domestic industry. Although the peril point cannot be regarded as more than an educated guess, our delegation is not authorized to offer concessions which would reduce rates below this level. Originally incorporated into the Act in 1948, the peril point was repealed in 1949 and reinstated in 1951.

Next, if after a concession is granted, a domestic industry feels injured by import competition, it can apply for relief under the escape clause. A positive determination by the Tariff Commission may lead to withdrawal of the concession if the President concurs with the Commission's recommendation. The clause first appeared in the 1951 extension of the Act, although it had in fact been incorporated in trade agreements since 1943. In each escape clause investigation, the Tariff Commission must make three successive determinations. First, it must define the scope of the industry to be covered by the investigation. Since the inability to measure cross elasticities precludes a precise definition of an industry, it is defined in the Act as producers "producing like or directly competitive products." While more explicit guidance could be provided on this point,[21] any definition would leave much of the decision to the discretion of the Commission. The segmentation rule followed by the Commission in the past has been subject to considerable criticism,[22] as it could lead to

---

[21]For example, the commission has asked Congress to specify whether only products that go on the free market should constitute the domestic industry, or if products which are made for one's self ("captive") should also be included.

[22]Professor Don Humphrey, testifying before the House Ways and Means Committee (*Hearings, op. cit.,* p. 402), suggested:

"Repeal the fragmentation amendment and base the test of serious injury on the industry's entire output. While some industries face increased foreign competition on certain products, they at the same time enjoy expanding exports and domestic markets in other products. It seems unfair to provide relief under the escape clause while the industry benefits from export markets created by the liberalization of some other industry's tariff.

As a general rule, no genuine hardship is involved so long as an industry can adjust to foreign competition by expanding some lines of output and contracting others.

To the contrary, the shift in the composition of output offers positive benefits, which raise the standard of living of the community, the nation, and the world. That is because the same resources are used to produce goods of greater value."

the use of the escape clause by an "industry" consisting of a few relatively inefficient producers.

Once the industry is defined, the Commission must determine whether or not serious injury took place. In interpreting the Act, the Commission tended to follow the "share of the market concept," requesting an industry seeking escape clause relief only to prove that its share of the market has declined because of increased imports. This criterion was often judged as too lenient,[23] since even an expanding industry can prove injury if imports captured a larger share of a rapidly growing market. Finally, there remains the difficult problem of tracing the "decline in share of the market" to the tariff concession. Import competing industries strongly object to the need for proving such a causal relation,[24] claiming that relief should be granted regardless of whether the increased import is due to an earlier tariff concession.

In the 1958 legislation, escape clause proceedings were expedited by granting subpoena power[25] to the Tariff Commission, by shortening the time allowed for investigation from nine to six months, and by

---

[23]Note, for example, the proposal of the National Council of American Importers made before the House Ways and Means Committee *(Hearings, op. cit.,* p. 1702):

"The word 'injury,' for the purpose of this section, shall mean a steady decline, over a representative period, in the sales volume, in the working force employed, and the profits of an industry economically and efficiently operated in the United States, directly caused by a rising trend of competitive imports which are similar in material, use, quality, texture, grade, and other physical characteristics, thus giving rise to a situation whereby such domestic industry is confronted with the actual necessity of making too rapid adjustments to avoid serious loss of capital: *Provided, however,* that such decline in sales, working force employed, and profits is not due, wholly or in part, to technological developments, style or fashion changes, or to other factors not related to said import competition."

[24]The difficulty faced by the Tariff Commission in ascertaining such causal relations may be illustrated by the lead and zinc industries. These industries were found by the Tariff Commission to have been injured by tariff concessions. Yet the *New York Times* of August 31, 1958 (financial section), quotes a leading producer of nonferrous metals as stating that "no reasonable tariff would enable domestic mines to operate competitively."

[25]Since most of the information on which escape clause decisions are based is gathered from the industry itself, the cooperation of all companies forming the industry is imperative. Partly because many producing companies also have substantial import interests, such cooperation has not always been forthcoming. Consequently, many investigations were either subject to delays, or completed with inadequate samples. In addition to minimizing such delays, the subpoena power would enable the Commission to conduct investigations upon applications by labor unions and other non-industry groups.

instructing the commission to initiate such proceedings whenever it finds in peril point[26] investigations that more restrictive customs treatment is necessary to prevent injury. A more restrictive provision was the increase in authority to raise tariffs whenever escape clause relief is granted. The 1958 Extension Act raised the maximum limit of such increases from 50 percent above the 1945 tariff level to 50 percent above the 1934 level. Within this authority, the President was permitted to convert specific duties existing in July, 1934, to their ad valorem equivalent in that year, and apply the 50 percent increase to the converted figure.[27] While permission to use quotas was retained, the President was authorized to impose up to 50 percent duty on commodities on the free list.

With respect to the Tariff Commission's determinations in escape clause investigations, the legislation permitted a narrow definition of industry thereby making it possible for a small segment of an industry to demonstrate injury even when the industry as a whole experienced prosperity and growth; and enabled domestic industries to base their claims for serious injury strictly on a decline in their share of the market even if absolute levels of production and employment were on the increase. Moreover, the 1958 extension introduced for the first time a breach in the President's authority for final decision in escape clause cases by authorizing a two-thirds majority of both Houses of Congress to override the President when he declines to accept a Tariff Commission recommendation.[28]

A final avenue of relief, also strenghtened in the 1950's, is the national security clause. Administered by the Office of Defense and Civilian Mobilization, it permits withdrawal of concessions in cases where the affected domestic industry is essential to national security.

It is thus abundantly clear that two main threads were woven through the reciprocal trade legislation. One was designed to liberalize imports into the United States, especially of industrial products, while the other was dedicated to the protection of American industry from

---

[26]Foreign nations have, in the past, been reluctant to consent to modifications of American tariff concessions following peril point findings. Escape clause relief, on the other hand, is an accepted procedure in international commercial agreements.

[27]This modification restores the effectiveness of specific duties which was impaired during the war and postwar inflation.

[28]Congressional consideration of such cases will be accorded a "highly privileged" status, and thus be expedited.

import competition. It is true that the escape clause has been invoked very sparingly in the past.[29] But this may have been a direct result of the noninjurious nature of the concessions and of the effective application of the peril point provision. It is reasonable to assume that many concessions constituted reductions in excess protection. Furthermore, the mere knowledge that the escape clause exists and may be applied if imports do injure a domestic industry, deters foreign exporters from establishing sales outlets in this country, particularly when those require considerable investments. The two general philosophies of the legislation, trade liberalization and "no injury" to domestic industry, are not reconcilable on economic grounds. But if political considerations are the motivating force behind U. S. commercial policies, they become compatible indeed. The offers of tariff concessions, for whatever political purpose, were designed in such a way as to minimize domestic injury. The product by product approach to negotiotions, coupled with the aforementioned provisions in the law, made that possible.

But toward the end of the 1950's the no-injury provisions were becoming increasingly incompatible with the main objectives of the legislation even for those who viewed the program strictly as a tool of foreign policy. The concessions granted by the United States during the past generation had more than halved the level of the tariff, a reduction which practically eliminated all the "excess protection" in the tariff structure. It was no longer possible to grant many concessions without inflicting injury on domestic industries, by simply curtailing the amount of "water" in the tariff. Any further reduction in the level of protection was almost certain to displace some domestic production. This was particularly true in some of the highly protected labor-intensive industries in whose markets our European trading partners had particular interests.

---

[29]The thousands of concessions granted throughout the history of the Program gave rise, up until the late 1950's, to only 87 escape clause investigations. Of these, tariff changes were recommended in 29 cases involving 26 commodities. The President, in turn, accepted the Commission's recommendation for nine commodities while for three commodities he took action other than tariff change to assist the industry. These statistics were taken by the administration as an indication of the non-injurious nature of the concessions. For a discussion of the Tariff Commission's decisions in escape clause cases, see I. Kravis "Trade Agreement Escape Clause," *American Economic Review*, June, 1954; and W. B. Kelly, "The Expanded Trade Agreements Escape Clause, 1955-61," *Journal of Political Economy*, February, 1962.

Regardless of its objective, any significant trade liberalization program in the next decade was likely to be injurious to domestic interests. An effective and strictly enforced escape clause, designed to prevent such injury, could have jeopardized the entire program. If tariff cuts were needed to strengthen the alliance or to expand American exports, they had to be granted at a sacrifice of some American production. (And inadvertently they would in the long run bring about the salutary economic effect of shifting domestic resources to more competitive industries.) Any means to prevent the inroads of foreign products in the American markets came into conflict with the policy of tariff liberalization.

TRADE ADJUSTMENT ASSISTANCE

Given an adequate growth rate, the resources displaced by increased imports could shift to industries in which the United States enjoys comparative advantage. But this process takes time. In the short run a number of workers, employers, and communities would be hurt. And in a society which assumes some responsibility for the economic well-being of its members such an impact of public policy could not be overlooked.

Legislators and public officials who were interested in continuing the program began to recognize the need for finding an acceptable substitute for tariff relief under the escape clause. If most Americans stood to benefit from the increased efficiency resulting from trade liberalization, a way had to be found to compensate those who would incur the short-run losses caused by displaced domestic production. Thus, support was gathering behind a program for trade adjustment assistance, which had been advocated by economists for quite some time.

Instead of protecting import-competing industries by the escape clause and thus perpetuating inefficiency, why not promote their transfer to lines of production in which they can compete effectively? The government can facilitate such movement of resources via a program designed to aid those who are injured by import competition.

Whenever the Tariff Commission would find, upon investigation, that an industry had been injured by import competition generated by a previous tariff concession, its recommendation need not be limited to tariff relief. Instead, it could recommend direct assistance. To employers the program could offer low interest loans, aid in research, market information, and other assistance in moving to new lines of production. To workers it would provide opportunities for retraining, and would offer to defray transport costs to new locations whenever necessary. And to communities injured by import competition, it would offer any assistance necessary to diversify the industrial base and adjust to the new circumstances. This avenue of relief has the added advantage of making it easier to administer the Act. Because of the narrow choice of action open to the President under previous legislation in cases of serious injury—action which involves modification of international obligations—the Tariff Commission had to be very rigid in recommending escape clause relief. The new method would make possible more liberal determinations.

It is because of these obvious merits of trade adjustment assistance that the proposed program began to receive serious public attention. For the first time in the postwar period it has also entered the political arena. While the 1960 Republican platform still advocated the escape clause mechanism for protecting domestic industries from serious injury, its Democratic counterpart pledged support for trade adjustment assistance to replace or at least supplement the escape clause. Thus the 1960 Republican platform[30] stated:

Carrying forward, under the Trade Agreements Act, the policy of gradual selective—and truly reciprocal—reduction of unjustifiable barriers to trade among free nations. We advocate effective administration of the Act's escape clause and peril point provisions to safeguard American jobs and domestic industries against serious injury.

At the same time, the Democratic platform specified:

World trade is more than ever essential to world peace. In the tradition of Cordell Hull, we shall expand world trade in every responsible way.

Since all Americans share the benefits of this policy its costs should not be the burden of a few. We shall support practical measures to ease the necessary adjustments of industries and communities which may be unavoidably hurt by increases in imports . . . .

The Democratic administration will help trade-affected industries by measures consistent with economic growth, orderly transition, fair competition, and the long-run strength of all parts of our nation.

Trade-affected industries and communities need and deserve appropriate help through trade adjustment measures such as direct loans, tax incentives, defense contracts priority, and retraining assistance.

---

[30]Partisan differences on this issue were not as clear cut as might appear from the platforms. Such influential members of the Republican Party as Senator Javits of New York declared themselves as staunch supporters of the Assistance Program and have proposed studies to estimate its scope.

C. The Trade Expansion Act of 1962

A trade adjustment program was embodied for the first time in the Trade Expansion Act of 1962. Indeed, this was one of several drastic departures from the earlier reciprocal trade legislations. Other liberal features included a vast increase in the President's tariff cutting authority. Under the new five-year act, the President was permitted to cut duties by up to 50 percent of their July, 1962, level, to remove altogether duties that did not exceed 5 percent on that date, and to eliminate duties on articles in which the United States and the EEC were responsible for at least 80 percent of aggregate exports.[31] Also subject to removal are duties on temperate and tropical zone agricultural commodities. Tariff negotiations were to be conducted on broad categories rather than on a product by product basis.

These major shifts can be traced to two alternative motives. The first possibility is that the political motive for the legislation is still the overwhelmingly strong one. Under this interpretation, the Act was a way of responding to the erosion of the American political leadership in Europe. Drastic tariff reductions were regarded as a vehicle to reassert the U. S. position through economic interdependence. The trade adjustment provision is no more than a recognition that this objective can no longer be pursued without injuring certain domestic interests; and the authority to eliminate tariff on tropical goods, on a reciprocal basis with the EEC, was regarded as a way to minimize EEC discrimination in favor of French Africa and against Latin America, an area in which there is a deep U. S. political interest. More generally, the Act was designed to minimize the political division in Europe and in the Western Alliance, which was generated by tariff discrimination between the two rival trade groups.

An alternative interpretation would place primary emphasis on economic considerations, and would suggest that the legislation has shifted from an essentially political to economic conception. Thus, trade liberalization is regarded as a means of attaining higher efficiency with the shift of resources to be facilitated by trade adjustment assistance. Likewise, the legislation reflects concern over the economic effects of EEC discrimination on American exports, and on the economic well-being of other countries. On both interpretations, the position and policies of the EEC occupy a pivotal role, and the current

---

[31]The effect of this provision is minimal because the 80 percent criterion encompasses very few products as long as Britain is not a member of the EEC.

round of GATT negotiations is widely regarded as mainly a United States–EEC bargaining session. (EFTA does not negotiate as one unit.)[32] In all probability both the economic and the political motives played a part in the formulation of the new Act.

It is under the authority of this legislation that the United States is negotiating in the Kennedy Round. But the high hopes originally held for this bargaining session are gradually giving way to more modest aspirations. The EEC is proving to be more inward then outward looking, and a change in this attitude seems unlikely. Agricultural protectionism appears to prevent any drastic expansion of trade in farm products. In the industrial field the negotiations are bogged down over the issues of tariff disparities[33] and the American selling price method of valuation of certain chemicals imported into the United States. In view of the exception lists tabled, the originally hoped-for 50 percent cut across the board was admittedly overly optimistic. At best, tough and prolonged bargaining lie ahead. At the time of writing, indications are that a 35 percent cut on industrial tariffs is still a realistic expectation, and that the Administration would ask for Congressional extension of the Act (which expires in mid-1967) for one or two years, so as to be able to complete the negotiations.[34] It is continuously emphasized in various quarters that failure of the Kennedy Round could bring about a complete reversal of the trend toward trade liberalization which has prevailed in the postwar period.

D. THE CHOICE AHEAD

Whatever the outcome of the Kennedy Round, it is likely that new concepts will have to be evolved to strengthen international trade relationships. The choice among available alternatives will probably rest mainly on political considerations. If, for example, the United States considers European unification and stability of overwhelming

---

[32]However, the four Nordic countries (Denmark, Finland, Norway and Sweden) have decided to negotiate as a unit in the final phase of the Kennedy Round. See IMF, *International Financial News Survey*, December 23, 1966, p. 1.

[33]See R. Baldwin "Tariff Cutting in the Kennedy Round," *Trade Growth and the Balance of Payments*, ed. Caves, Johnson and Kenen, (New York: Rand McNally, 1965), pp. 68-81.

[34]See the *Wall Street Journal*, December 16, 1966, pp. 22 and 12, the *New York Times*, December 18, 1966, Financial Section, pp. 1 and 9, and the *New York Times*, January 16, 1967, p. C-54.

importance, she would promote a trade union within Europe even at the expense of American "presence" on the continent, and of tariff discrimination against North America. This country might, in such a case, wish to compensate Japan and/or Canada, who would also be discriminated against, by giving them freer access to the American market. The possibility of a U. S.-Canadian free trade area comes to mind in this connection. On the other hand, should the United States consider its leadership and influence to be of fundamental importance, this country would be less willing to compromise its presence in Europe, and would oppose any policies which would discriminate against its exports, or which would weaken Atlantic political interdependence. Needless to emphasize, whatever the American objective, the outcome of any negotiations toward its attainment depends to a large extent on the attitude of the European powers, and primarily the EEC.

What, then, are the concrete alternatives? Perhaps the most radical departure from present trade arrangements would be the creation of an Atlantic Free Trade Area (AFTA). Encompassing North America, Japan, and Western Europe, AFTA would increase considerably the political and economic bonds of the alliance, and because of its irreversibility, would involve a far deeper commitment than a simple decision to reduce tariffs. Of late, a discussion of possible AFTA has penetrated the political arena, and the arrangement has also been proposed by the Canadian-American Committee (sponsored by the National Planning Association in the United States and the Private Planning Association of Canada) and the International Economic Policy Association of the United States.[35] As envisaged here, AFTA would remove all tariffs on trade in industrial products among the participants, but each member country would retain its own national tariff against outsiders. AFTA would call for only limited agreement of domestic economic policies, and the Common Market could join it as one unit.

It is possible, and even likely, that AFTA would prove unattractive to the EEC. Community members are certain to fear the dilution of their unity, and the French may not wish to compromise their leadership in the EEC. Nor is the French attitude likely to change after De Gaulle's departure from the political scene. In such a case, the United States could sponsor an AFTA without the EEC, involving

---

[35]See the *New York Times*, June 14, 1966.

mutual discrimination between the two groups. Although the door would be left open for the EEC to join at a later date, this arrangement could well lead to hardening of the division in the Atlantic alliance. It would also present Britain and some of its EFTA members with a difficult choice: to throw their lot with the United States,[36] or to attempt once again, without assurance of success, to join the EEC. Perhaps in the end they might opt for the first alternative.

Another more modest policy would involve continuation of Kennedy Round type negotiations, under the unconditional MFN principle, in the hope that a 50 percent or more tariff cut would eventually be realized. Alternatively, the United States and its allies could attempt to negotiate a "low tariff club," calling for drastic tariff reduction (but not elimination) subject only to the conditional MFN clause. This, of course, would violate the current principles of GATT.

All the trade arrangements mentioned above would be restricted to manufactures, because it is not conceivable that the industrial countries would relinquish the protection of their agricultural sector.

In most of the industrial countries, foodstuffs are subject to nontariff measures, the effects of which are difficult to quantify. In the case of foodstuffs, present trade patterns reflect the application of fixed and variable duties, subsidies, and quantitative restrictions in the importing countries; and the use of price support measures by several of the major exporters. Consequently, the possible effects of easing the level of protection can hardly be foreseen. In addition, given the political and social issues involved in the protection of domestic agriculture (resulting in subsidies and price support programs in most industrial countries), it may be difficult to substantially alter the policies currently applied, and one can hardly speculate on the form that changes in these policies would take. Similar considerations apply to certain fuels where modifications in the system of protection would necessitate a reappraisal of energy policies. On the other hand, the protection of industrial materials and manufactured goods takes largely the form of tariffs, and these commodities have

---

[36]Recently, a prominent British industrialist (the chairman of Imperial Chemical Industries, Ltd.) warned against Britain entering a Free Trade Area with the United States and Canada even if it fails to join the EEC. "The danger for Britain is that what may be called partnership may in reality be absorption, and that Britain might become a satellite." He advocated a European orientation for the U. K. no matter what happens at the common market negotiations. See *The Wall Street Journal,* January 20, 1967, p. 5.

been in the center of trade negotiations during the postwar period.

In fact, the trend since World War II has been to intensify the protection of domestic agriculture (the common agricultural policy of the EEC is the most recent indication of this phenomenon); and to apply quantitative restrictions to the imports of petroleum and its products in the United States, and to coal in the countries of Western Europe. At the same time, trade in industrial materials and manufactures has been increasingly liberalized, and the obstacles to further liberalization do not appear to be unsurmountable. An Atlantic Free Trade Area can be regarded as a final and most drastic step in this direction.

In all probability, the proposals outlined above would not be welcomed by the less developed countries. Any degree of trade liberalization among the industrial nations, not subject to the unconditional most favored nations clause, would discriminate against them, and they are likely to view it as a "rich men's club." And this precisely at a time when these nations are demanding in UNCTAD[37] preferential treatment for their manufactured exports. The United States and its major European allies could hardly ignore such resentment on the part of the developing nations, and some arrangement would have to be made to accommodate or compensate them.

Short of emphasizing that the decision among the possible alternatives will essentially be political in nature, this study will not attempt any further elaboration on their political effects. Rather it will be confined to what economists have traditionally regarded as their proper function: An assessment of the effects of alternative policies on the American economy. For although the final choice would be based mainly on political consideration, the decision makers would wish to know in advance the economic implications of the policies among which they must choose.

---

[37]United Nations Conference on Trade and Development.

Part II

Effect of Alternative Trade Arrangements on the U. S. Balance of Trade

PART II

Effect of Alternative Trade Arrangements on the U. S. Balance of Trade

In the present context, an Atlantic Free Trade Area (AFTA) implies the elimination of tariff and quota restrictions on trade in manufactured products between North America, Western Europe, and Japan. Chapter 1 utilized the Bureau of the Census definition of manufactured products encompassing divisions 20-39 of the Standard Industrial Classification. This definition has the advantage of permitting direct comparisons of commodity trade with domestic production and consumption. However, since this study considers the relationship between the United States and other countries, it is necessary to define manufactured products in a way which would make possible intercountry comparisons. The trade figures of all the nations participating in the proposed AFTA are reported quarterly and annually according to the three- and five-digit Standard International Trade Classification (SITC), by the United Nations and the OECD.[1] Sections 5-8 of the SITC include the items generally considered as manufactures: chemicals (section 5), machinery and transport equipment (section 7), manufactured products classified chiefly

---

[1]Organization for Economic Cooperation and Development. It is anticipated that in the next few years production figures of all industrial nations will be available within the same framework. Also, the U. S. Census Bureau is currently engaged in developing a conversion system between the SIC and the SITC.

by material (section 6, with the exception of groups 682.1-689.1),[2] and other manufactures (section 8). Roughly speaking, this definition corresponds to SIC divisions 22-28 and 30-39, i.e., it excludes divisions 19-21, and 29. Also excluded are some items in divisions 24, 26, and 33, which are regarded as crude materials by the SITC.[3]

Total U. S. exports of manufactured products in 1960 amounted to $12.6 billions, while imports were $5.8 billion. AFTA,[4] however, takes only half of total manufacturing exports, and is the source of about 90 percent of U. S. industrial imports.[5] The year 1960 was selected as the base year because the discriminatory effects of the EEC and EFTA were not appreciable at that time. We shall consider separately the direct effect of trade liberalization on U. S. trade flows, and the effect of eliminating European discrimination against nonmember states.

---

[2]These are the unwrought, non-ferrous base metals.

[3]An example is the commodity "Pulp mill products" (SIC No. 2611), which is classified under SITC No. 251, ("wood pulp").

[4]Includes Western Europe, Canada, and Japan.

[5]See: OECD *Statistical Bulletins,* Foreign Trade—Series C, "Trade by Commodities, Export and Import, 1959-1962."

Chapter 3

Effect of an Atlantic Free Trade Area on American Imports

The direct effect of AFTA on U. S. imports depends on the height of the tariff to be eliminated, on the export-supply elasticities in the supplying countries, and on the import-demand elasticities in the United States. These variables will be examined in turn.

A. U. S. TARIFF

The main method of protection employed by the United States in the industrial sector of the economy is the tariff. (For a discussion of quotas see section E below.) An extensive literature exists on the structure of the American tariff, the extent of the protection it affords, and the effect of the reciprocal tariff reductions on American imports.[6] While no useful purpose would be served by summarizing these analyses, it should be noted that the U. S. tariff schedule covers about 6,000 commodities, and that in the early 1960's about 38 percent of all imports entered the country duty free. This percentage ranged

---

[6]For some recent contributions see: (a) *Foreign Trade Policy,* Compendium of papers on United States Foreign Trade Policy, Sub-committee on Foreign Trade Policy, Committee on Ways and Means, Washington, 1958, pp. 211-302: (b) Howard Piquet, *Trade, Aid and the Tariff,* Thomas Y. Crowell, 1953; (c) Don Humphrey, *American Imports,* New York, 1955; (d) L. B. Krause, "United States Imports and the Tariff," *American Economic Review,* Proceedings May, 1959, pp. 542-51; (e) M. E. Kreinin, "Effect of Tariff Changes on the Prices and Volume of Imports," *American Economic Review,* June, 1961, pp. 310-24.

from a high of 84 in the crude foodstuffs category to a low of 2 among manufactured foodstuffs. The percentage of finished manufactures imports entering duty free was close to 30 (Appendix II-A).

With a few major exceptions, tariff rates tend to vary directly with the degree of processing or fabrication to which the merchandise has been subjected. Manufactured goods, therefore, tend to fall within the middle and higher duty brackets. Indeed, B. Vaccara estimated the degree of protection of 311 SIC manufacturing industries, and concluded that "manufacturing is primarily a protected activity in the United States' economy." [7]

Several transformations of the published tariff rates are necessary before their effect on trade flows can be estimated. First, specific rates must be converted into ad valorem equivalents in order to make them comparable to each other.

Secondly, nominal tariff rates need to be converted to effective rates; namely related to value added rather than to gross value of output (which includes imported materials), allowance being made for tariffs on imported materials. For while nominal tariffs apply to the total value of imports, they protect only the portion of that value produced in the home country. At the same time, the level of protection accorded the production of a final good is also affected by the level of duty on imported inputs used in the production process. Thus an increase in the rate of duty levied on imported materials would lower the degree of effective protection accorded to the final good produced with these materials, even if the nominal tariff on the latter remained unchanged. The effective protective rate is the percentage increase in value added per unit in an economic activity which is made possible by the tariff structure relative to the situation in the absence of tariffs but with the same exchange rate. In a simple case where commodity j is subject to a nominal import duty (T_j), and uses one imported input i on which the tariff is (T_i), the value added per unit on j in the absence of a tariff is:

$$v_j = p_j(1 - a_{ij})$$

and the value added per unit of j made possible by the tariff structure is:

$$v'_j = p_j [(1 + T_j) - a_{ij}(1 + T_i)]$$

where (p_j) is the price of a unit of j in the absence of tariffs and

[7]Beatrice N. Vaccara, *Employment and Output in Protected Manufacturing Industries* (Washington, D. C.: The Brookings Institution, 1960), p. 22.

(a_{ij}) is the share of i in the cost of j in the absence of tariffs. The effective protective rate is:[8]

$$(1)\quad G_j = \frac{v'_j - v_j}{v_j} = \frac{p_j\,[(1+T_j) - a_{ij}(1+T_i) - (1-a_{ij})]}{p_j(1-a_{ij})} = \frac{T_j - a_{ij}T_i}{1 - a_{ij}}$$

If, for example, the nominal tariff on a final consumer good is 20 percent, while the duty levied on imported materials which constitute one half of its value is only 10 percent, the effective rate of protection on the final good is 30 percent. Suppose now that as a result of multilateral negotiations, tariff rates on final products are cut by 25 percent, while those applied to primary and intermediate products remain unchanged. The nominal rate on commodity j would become 15 percentage points. But the effective tariff would decline from 30 to 20 percentage points—a reduction of $33\frac{1}{3}$ percent. On the other hand, if the imported input i is also included in the overall reduction, the rate on j would decline only to 22.5 percentage points— namely by 25 percent. More generally, assuming no change in (a_{ij})[9] the "total differential" of (G_j) will be the change in effective protection for any given changes in (T_j) and (T_i):

$$\Delta G_j \approx \frac{1}{1 - a_{ij}}\,\Delta T_j - \frac{a_{ij}}{1 - a_{ij}}\Delta T_i\,\bullet$$

Divide through by ΔT_j

$$\frac{\Delta G_j}{\Delta T_j} = \frac{1}{1 - a_{ij}} - \frac{a_{ij}\bullet\Delta T_i}{(1 - a_{ij})\Delta T_j} = \frac{1}{1 - a_{ij}}\left(1 - \frac{a_{ij}\bullet\Delta T_i}{\Delta T_j}\right)$$

From this we have:

$$\frac{\Delta G_j}{\Delta T_j} \gtreqless 1 \text{ if: } \frac{1}{1 - a_{ij}}\left(1 - \frac{a_{ij}\Delta T_i}{\Delta T_j}\right) \gtreqless 1;$$

$$\text{or } 1 - \frac{a_{ij}\bullet\Delta T_i}{\Delta T_j} \gtreqless 1 - a_{ij}; \text{ or } -\frac{\Delta T_i}{\Delta T_j} \gtreqless -1$$

We conclude that:

$$\frac{\Delta G_j}{\Delta T_j} \gtreqless 1 \text{ if } \frac{\Delta T_j}{\Delta T_i} \gtreqless 1.$$

In words, the change in the effective tariff on the final commodity will exceed or fall short of the change in the nominal rate applied to

---

[8]For the development, discussion and extension of this formula see W. M. Corden, "The Structure of a Tariff System and the Effective Protective Rate," *Journal of Political Economy*, June, 1966, pp. 221-37.

[9]One of the necessary refinements in the theory of effective protection is modification of the assumption of fixed input coefficients.

it, depending on whether or not the change in the nominal tariff on the final good exceeds the change in duty imposed on the imported inputs.

Also, in order for the effective rate to remain unchanged, we must have

$$\frac{1}{1 - a_{ij}} \Delta T_j = \frac{a_{ij}}{1 - a_{ij}} \Delta T_i \text{ or } \frac{\Delta T_j}{\Delta T_i} = a_{ij}.$$

Industrial countries tend to levy higher tariffs on finished manufactures than on raw materials and intermediate goods. Correspondingly, the effective rates in the manufacturing sector are considerably higher than the nominal rates. Indeed for several countries or country-groups (U. S., U. K., EEC, Sweden, and Japan) the differences between the two rates are often between 50 and 80 percent.[10] It should be noted that while the production cost of the tariff (i.e., shift of resources from low to more highly protected industries) depends on the effective rate, the consumption effect (shift of consumers from highly to less protected final consumption goods) depends on the nominal rate. Unfortunately, it is not possible to use effective tariffs in this study. First, estimates of such rates are not available for Canada and several other nations which are important for U. S. trade. Even the rates calculated for the aforementioned countries were not computed at the desired level of disaggregation. Second, and more importantly, this study is concerned mainly with elimination or reduction of tariffs on goods in categories 5-8 SITC. Many of them enter as inputs into the productive processes of other products in these categories. Thus a given across the board tariff reduction (or elimination) would lower effective protection by more than the cut in nominal rates, although not by the full amount implied in unchanged protection of inputs. Since we do not know exactly the product mix affected by any policy change, it would be impossible to determine the change in effective rates. However, the above formulas suggest that the use of nominal rates would lead to an underestimation of the effect of commercial policy changes on trade flows.

Third, it is necessary to aggregate the published tariff rates to a manageable number of commodity groups, common to all AFTA

[10]See Bela Balassa, "Tariff Protection Industrial Countries: An Evaluation," *Journal of Political Economy*, December, 1955, pp. 573-94. For another empirical study see G. Basevi, "The U. S. Tariff Structure: Estimates of Effective Rates of Protection of U. S. Industries and Industrial Labor," *Review of Economics and Statistics*, May, 1966, pp. 147-60.

countries, which can also be readily related to trade statistics. In such a transformation, each rate should ideally be weighted by what imports would have been in the absence of tariffs. But since this information is not known, some other weighting procedure must be devised. One often-used measure of aggregation is the tariff rates weighted by value of the country's own imports. For the second half of the 1950's, this has been estimated at 11 percent for the United States, 19 percent for Japan, 17 percent for the United Kingdom, 15 percent for France, and 9 percent for Germany.[11] On this measure the United States is usually considered average in its degree of protection. But this method of aggregation, which uses import values of individual commodities as weights, invariably underestimates the protective effect of the tariff. Since the highly protected products with very restrictive or even prohibitive duty receive little or no weight, they are hardly represented in the computation.

This problem may be particularly severe in the case of the United States, and probably leads to a larger understatement of the level of protection than in other countries, because the distribution of American tariff rates shows a higher degree of asymmetry and a larger number of high (and presumably very restrictive) rates, than is the case in most European countries. Of 3,760 rates on industrial products examined recently by the EEC Commission,[12] the United States has 325 items taxed at 41 percent and over, compared to 62 in the United Kingdom, and none in the Common Market.

Indeed, perusal of a recent study by the Committee for Economic Development[13] shows the powerful downward bias imparted by the import weighting technique. In that study all Schedule A products are presented with their attendant tariff rates and classified according to the five-digit SITC. Then a tariff average is computed for each SITC group from the constituent Schedule A commodities, weighted by 1960 imports. In many cases, the small weights on high duty items reduces drastically the level of the tariff so computed. This phenomenon is further reflected in Appendix Table II-A. The reduction in

---

[11]*Trade Restraints in the Western Community,* Subcommittee on Foreign Economic Policy of the Joint Economic Committee, United States Congress, Washington, 1961.

[12]*Disparate Aspects of Selected Tariff Structures,* The European Economic Community, Brussels, p. 12. (Mimeographed.)

[13]F. K. Topping, *Comparative Tariffs and Trade,* Committee on Economic Development, March, 1963.

the rates of duty in the United States since the 1930's, as shown in the last column, resulted in a decrease (rather than an increase) in the proportion of products entering duty free. This decline has taken place in all commodity classes with the exception of crude food-stuffs. It shows that as tariffs are reduced the amount of dutiable imports rises. Likewise, the ratio of duty to total imports has *increased* somewhat during the postwar period.

As an alternative, one could weigh each tariff rate by the combined world imports of the commodity, or by total imports into the industrial countries. However, inasmuch as the tariff structure of the major importing countries is quite similar, the same bias would be imparted by this approach, although to a lesser degree. It has also been suggested that the proper weight is total consumption (imports plus domestic production) of the product in the country. But aside from the fact that tariff classifications do not coincide with class-fications of production or consumption statistics (making this approach impractical), the weights proposed here are also affected by the tariff rates. In order to avoid this bias, unweighted averages— namely, arithmetic averages of the tariff rates—have been proposed as a solution. However, such averages do not give expression to the relative importance of individual commodities in the trade of the industrial countries.

It is apparent that there exists no satisfactory way of estimating the overall level of a country's tariff, or of aggregating tariff rates over major commodity categories. Each method has biases of its own. The conceptual problem is compounded by the practical need for tariff rates covering comparable product groups in all industrial countries, groups which must correspond to the classification employed in reporting trade statistics. The choice must therefore be made not only on grounds of principle, but also on pragmatic considerations relating to the ready availability of data.

In order to minimize (but by no means eliminate) the conceptual problem, and to achieve intercountry comparability, a recent P.E.P. report[14] has converted the tariff rates of all countries in the Atlantic community to a common structure, using a single list of subdivisions. Specifically, all commodities entering international trade were classified under the 1,100 main headings (forming 99 chapters) of the Brussels

---

[14]See, Political and Economic Planning, *Atlantic Tariffs and Trade* (London: George Allen and Unwin, 1962).

Tariff Nomenclature (BTN), which now corresponds to the new SITC; and ad valorem duty rates were presented for each item.[15]

In the large European countries most tariff rates are ad valorem. On the other hand, the United States and Canada, along with five small European countries, employ a large number of specific duties. Such duties were converted to their ad valorem equivalent, using 1958 unit value of imports (no conversion was made for items in which there was no trade in a recent year).[16] Next, unweighted averages were computed by the P.E.P. for each of the 85 three-digit SITC industries within sections 5-8.

As these figures were computed for almost all the countries in the projected AFTA, they form the basic tariff data used in this study. But estimates based on tariff rates weighted by the combined imports of the industrial countries will also be presented for comparative purposes. Two adjustments were made in the case of the United States. First, since U. S. duties are based on f.o.b. valuation of imported commodities, they were reduced by 10 percent,[17] so as to conform to their European counterparts where c.i.f. valuation is used; and second, an upward adjustment of the American tariff was made in the case of certain chemical imports, to account for the "American selling price" method of valuation.[18]

---

[15]For an extensive discussion comparing the U. S. and the EEC tariff rates, see Committee for Economic Development, *Trade Negotiations For a Better Free World Economy*, Appendix B, pp. 67-85.

[16]The rates so converted usually understate the protective effect of specific duties for the following reason: Import headings may cover several kinds of goods, or there may be variations in the value of the same kind within one import heading (e.g., reflecting variations in quality or different sources of supply). Since specific duties are more effective in keeping out lower-price imports, they tend to raise the average value of imports and lower the equivalent converted ad valorem rates. In the case of the United States, the underestimation problem was largely avoided because of the refinement of the import classifications. Schedule A often has sub-headings for a number of ranges of value of an imported commodity. Thus any specific duty could be converted into its percentage equivalent more nearly comparable with ad valorem rates. This, however, is not the case in Canada, where some understatement probably did take place.

[17]See K. F. Toping, *Comparative Tariffs and Trade*, Committee for Economic Development, March, 1963, p. XIII. See also the results of the Department of Commerce and the U. S. Tariff Commission studies, reported in: "C.i.f. v. F.o.b.." *Trade Talk*, Committee for a National Trade Policy, January-February, 1967.

[18]See, U. S. Tariff Commission, *Imports of Coal Tar Products*, Washington, July, 1964.

B. U. S. Import Prices

How would the removal of the tariff on industrial products affect the U. S. import prices? Two conflicting views are relevant here. On the one hand it might be argued that import prices would not be affected at all. Most industrial imports have close domestic substitutes, and in most cases the imports constitute a very small portion of total new supply. Consequently, import prices simply fall under the "umbrella" of domestic prices, and if tariffs were eliminated, the foreign supplier rather than the domestic consumer would reap the benefit. This view, which is consistent with the "charging what the traffic would bear" philosophy, may be valid for standardized products, where quality, brand names, and other features of product differentiation are absent or immaterial. But manufactures are highly differentiated commodities. Even identical goods produced here and abroad are not considered perfect substitutes for each other. And often there are variations in quality, specifications, and the like. In all such instances the umbrella price argument does not apply.

An opposite assumption is that import prices fully reflect the tariff, and under AFTA, they would be reduced by the full amount of the tariff. This view implies that export supply curves in the exporting countries are infinitely elastic; that is, that every country can expand production at constant cost. Indeed such an assumption is made explicitly or implicitly in most contributions dealing with the effect of mutilateral or unilateral tariff changes.[19]

But neither a priori reasoning nor empirical evidence justify this presumption with respect to most of America's trading partners. The elasticity of export supply depends on domestic supply and demand elasticities and on the share of exports in domestic production. In most European countries foreign sales account for a substantial proportion of production. Consequently they cannot be expected to expand exports considerably at constant costs.

AFTA however does not involve an unbalanced expansion of exports. The multilateral elimination (or reduction) of tariffs would increase imports as well as exports, and the relevant question is

---

[19]See H. G. Johnson, "The Gains from Freer Trade With Europe: An Estimate," *Manchester School*, September, 1958, pp. 247-55; L. B. Krause, "United States Imports and the Tariff," *American Economic Review*, May, 1959, pp. 542-51; and R. M. Stern "The U. S. Tariff and the Efficiency of the U. S. Economy," *American Economic Review*, May, 1964, p. 463.

whether the reallocation of resources (from import-competing to export industries) can be carried out without raising export prices. If we consider that factors are employed in different proportions in the two types of industries, and that there are technical limitations on factor substitution, it is plausible that the reallocation would necessitate changes in relative prices. This is particularly true in cases of extremely tight labor market conditions, such as those prevailing in Europe—conditions which are expected to continue in the foreseeable future.[20] Wages in the export industries would have to be raised in order to bid away resources from other sectors of the economy. Under noncompetitive factor (and product) markets, such increases are not likely to be reversible. These effects are likely to be counteracted to some extent by the increased efficiency of the economy as resources are shifted from low productivity import-competing industries to high productivity export industries. Also, as capacity expands in the long run, cost curves may flatten out somewhat.

The actual behavior of export prices in the event of trade liberalization probably lies somewhere between the two extreme assumptions examined above. The answer must be determined by empirical observations rather than by a priori reasoning. In studying the effects of the reciprocal tariff concessions granted by the United States during the 1955 and 1956 GATT negotiations,[21] I estimated that between one-third and one-half of the tariff cuts were passed on to the American consumer in the form of reduced import prices. The remaining gain was reaped by the foreign exporters through an increase in export prices. These were the results of tariff cuts averaging 15 percent. For the complete elimination of duties contemplated here, leading to a sharper increase in demand for foreign products, it is reasonable to expect a cut in import prices amounting to no more than one-third of the tariff. Indeed, more recently it has been noted that consumers benefited little from tariff reductions among EFTA countries.[22] However, on the supposition that the pressure on the European productive

---

[20]See Walter Salant *et al., The United States Balance of Payments in 1968* (known as the Brookings Study), Joint Economic Committee, United States Congress, Washington, 1963, pp. 50-53.

[21]See M. E. Kreinin, "Effect of Tariff Changes on the Value and Volume of Imports," *American Economic Review,* June, 1961, pp. 310-24.

[22]See *EFTA Reporter,* June 26, 1964, p. 4. However a subsequent more comprehensive (still unpublished) study by EFTA showed that most of the tariff cuts were reflected in import prices.

capacity may abate somewhat in the more distant future, I shall assume that one-half of the decline in duties will be reflected in import prices.[23] In addition, in order to show how sensitive the results are to this assumption, alternative estimates will be presented, where import prices are assumed to decline by the full amount of the tariff.

C. U. S. ELASTICITY OF DEMAND FOR IMPORTS

The effect of price reduction on the volume of imports depends on the elasticity of U. S. demand for industrial imports. It should be stated at the outset that even apart from any statistical considerations,[24] most calculated elasticities may understate the actual responsiveness of imports to tariff changes, because of the existence of prohibitive rates. Even when the tariff is highly restrictive, it still leaves room for some observed imports which can be incorporated into the elasticity computations. But when it is completely prohibitive, no such observations exist. This limitation applies more to American imports than to our exports, because very high (and presumably prohibitive) duties are more prevalent in the United States than in the major European countries. Examination of these so-called "non-performance items" revealed that while some are obsolete products which would not move even in the absence of a tariff, others may respond strongly to tariff reduction. This response is not reflected in the elasticities computed from observed data. The only way to incorporate it in the estimates is by relying on projections of commodity experts, rather than on observations of past experience. Because no quantitative estimates are available on the effect of the prohibitive rates, the deficiency cannot be overcome. It can only be borne in mind as we use the computed elasticities, and perhaps adjusted for in a few selected instances.

On the other hand, high tariffs may be levied on products in which the United States enjoys a comparative advantage, and their elimination would not result in the increase in imports anticipated by the "mechanistic" application of elasticity and tariff changes to 1960

---

[23]Although this assumption appears most reasonable to me, one may experiment with several variations of it. For example, it might be assumed that import prices would decline by two-thirds of the duty, or that the projected increases in export prices apply only to European sources of supply.

[24]See Guy H. Orcutt, "Measurement of Price Elasticities in International Trade," *The Review of Economics and Statistics,* May, 1950, pp. 117-32.

imports. Comparative advantage is a dynamic concept, and may not be reflected in the static position of an industry in 1960.

Accepting the factor proportions theory of international trade, and treating the United States as a relatively capital-abundant country, the relationship between tariff rates and comparative advantage can be examined by correlating tariffs with the labor intensity or cost of production in manufacturing industries. As the following quotation suggests, this correlation was traditionally thought to be positive:

the height of duty tends as a general rule to vary roughly with the ratio of direct labor costs to total costs in the industry performing the final stages of fabrication. Rates applicable to the complex products of our mass-production manufacturing industries are distinctly more moderate, on the whole, than those on goods produced by labor intensive industries, particularly where the production process is characterized by skilled artisanship, rather than advanced engineering technique.[25]

This supposition was verified by Vaccara,[26] who reached her conclusions by observing how labor intensity changes throughout the five categories of increasing protection into which her sample of industries was divided. But her index of protection was based on nominal tariff rates. Using "effective" rates, Basevi[27] found no clear relationship between the two variables for 1954, but a negative relation for 1958. Likewise, Vaccara's finding of a positive correlation between labor cost coefficients and protection was reversed when effective rather than nominal rates were employed as a measure of protection.

In another attempt this author failed to find any strong correlation between various types of tariff rates on the one hand, and an export share index of comparative advantage on the other.[28] (The derivation of the export share index is explained in Chapter 11 below.) The test was carried out for several industrial countries including the United States.

The relation between protection and comparative advantage appears rather inconclusive, and if anything—positive, leaving the question posed earlier (concerning the usefulness of the "mechanistic"

[25]*Foreign Trade Policy,* Compendium (1958), *op. cit.,* p. 213.

[26]B. Vaccara, *Employment and Output in Protected Manufacturing Industries* (Washington: The Brookings Institution, 1960).

[27]G. Basevi, "The United States Tariff Structure: Estimates of Effective Rates of Protection of United States Industries and Industrial Labor," *Review of Economics and Statistics,* May, 1966, pp. 147-60.

[28]See M. E. Kreinin "On the Restrictive Effect of the Tariff," *The Manchester School,* January, 1966, pp. 75-80.

approach) unresolved. We shall return to it in Chapter 11 in discussing the results. In the meantime, it should be borne in mind that the United States tariff today is in part the outcome of thirty years of selective tariff reductions subject to escape clause and peril point provisions. Under such circumstances it is likely that most rates have been lowered to a level somewhere around the threshhold of injury to the domestic industry.

A final limitation on the application of elasticity estimates to price changes arises from the possibility of price response. Domestic producers in specific industries may react to the tariff cut by lowering their prices in order to meet foreign competition, thereby barring (or at least moderating) any increase in imports. This, however, is unlikely to occur in the case of the United States, since imports occupy too small a share of total production in most industries. In the very few industries where imports play a major role—some price reduction may be expected.[29] But even here it is constrained by cost considerations since these tend to be labor intensive industries. With respect to American exports (the subject of the next chapter) this possibility can also be largely discounted on the ground that in most AFTA markets, industrialists are operating at capacity, and would not be inclined to react in this manner. Thus, while a sharp price response may occur in isolated instances, it can be safely ruled out as a general phenomenon applying to United States trade.

In previous contributions, two general approaches have been used for deriving elasticities of import demand—a direct and an indirect procedure. The former relies on the statistical estimation of import demand elasticities from data on imports, incomes, and prices or, alternatively, utilizes information provided by commodity experts. By contrast, the latter derives an estimate of import demand elasticities on the basis of information on elasticities of domestic demand and supply and the share of imports in domestic consumption and production.

---

[29]A recent study of steel imports has shown that even when imports made substantial inroads into the domestic market, the domestic producers did not lower prices to meet competition: "Summing up, there was no correlation between the proportion of imports to domestic open market consumption and the degree of price response. Wire rod and wire prices moved perversely to rising imports. Chain link fence and welded wire fabric prices tumbled, though imports were inconsequential. The apparent paradox, we submit, can be explained only by the structure of the industry." See W. Adams & J. B. Dirlam "Steel Imports and Vertical Integration," *American Economic Review,* September, 1964.

The formula employed in the indirect model is $\eta_m = (O_d/O_m)\,e_d + (O_s/O_m)e_s$, where O_d refers to domestic consumption, O_s to domestic supply and O_m to imports, while e_d and e_s are the domestic price elasticity of demand and supply, and η_m the import demand elasticity. The proposition follows from the fact that import-demand is the difference between domestic demand and domestic supply at various prices. Thus, the equation for import demand elasticity is [employing (d) to denote a small change]:

$$\eta_m = \frac{-P}{O_d - O_s} \cdot \frac{d(O_d - O_s)}{dP} = \left(\frac{-P}{O_d - O_s}\right) \cdot \left(\frac{dO_d}{dP}\right) - \left(\frac{P}{O_d - O_s}\right) \cdot \left(-\frac{dO_s}{dP}\right) = -\frac{P\frac{dO_d}{dP}}{O_d - O_s} + \frac{P\frac{dO_s}{dP}}{O_d - O_s}$$

Multiplying and dividing the first component by O_d, and the second component by O_s, we obtain:

$$\eta_m = \frac{-P/O_d \cdot \frac{dO_d}{dP}O_d}{O_d - O_s} + \frac{P/O_s \cdot \frac{dO_s}{dP}O_s}{O_d - O_s} = \frac{O_d}{O_d - O_s}e_d + \frac{O_s}{O_d - O_s}e_s = \left(\frac{O_d}{O_m}\right)e_d + \left(\frac{O_s}{O_m}\right)e_s$$

This relation has been used by Stern in estimating possible changes in American imports following an elimination of tariffs, and by J. E. Floyd in appraising the effects of a devaluation of the dollar on trade flows.[30] There are, however, serious problems with the application of this method. To begin with, while estimates on domestic demand elasticities are available for various categories of consumer goods and a few intermediate products in the United States and the United Kingdom, little is known of the elasticity of demand for investment goods which account for an important part of international trade. In other industrial countries, estimates for consumer goods are also scarce. At the same time, there are but few estimates of domestic supply elasticities of nonagricultural commodities. Also, the comparability of trade and production (consumption) statistics can be established only in the case of the United States.

However, the direct estimation of import demand elasticities has deficiencies of its own. The difficulties and error possibilities of estimation[31] suggest that the estimates obtained by the use of least-squares

---

[30]Robert M. Stern, "The U. S. Tariff and the Efficiency of the U. S. Economy," *American Economic Review*, Papers and Proceedings, May 1964, pp. 459-70. J. E. Floyd, "The Overvaluation of the Dollar," *The American Economic Review*, March, 1965, pp. 95-106.

[31]For example, see Guy H. Orcutt, "Measurement of Price Elasticities in International Trade," *Review of Economics and Statistics*, May, 1950, pp. 117-32, and Arnold C. Harberger, "A Structural Approach to the Problem of Import Demand," *American Economic Review*, May, 1953, pp. 148-59.

method generally have a downward bias, while no way has been devised to measure the size of this bias.

As to actual estimates,[32] in the case of the United States the recent calculations of Ball and Marwah appear to be the most reliable.[33] These authors applied regression analysis to quarterly data covering eleven postwar years and estimated import demand elasticities for five commodity groups, three of which are relevant for our discussion: −0.26 for crude materials, −1.38 for semimanufactures, and −3.50 for finished manufactures.

Another procedure has been applied by M. E. Kreinin[34] and L. B. Krause.[35] Kreinin compared data for two groups of commodities, classified according to whether or not they have been subject to tariff reductions. The elasticities implicit in his results are −5 for commodities excluding textiles[36] in the period 1954-56 and −6 for finished manufactures in the period 1955-59. In turn, in a cross section analysis of 91 categories of manufactured goods, Krause obtained "tariff" elasticity estimates of −5.6 for the period 1947-54, and −4.5 for 1947-58, while the elasticity of −0.5, estimated for 1954-58, was not statistically significant.[37] At the same time, with the exception of the latter period, the elasticity of demand for imports calculated with respect to the tariff change was considerably higher than the elasticities calculated with respect to price.[38]

[32]For a summary of studies see H. S. Cheng, *A Collection of Statistical Estimates of Elasticities in International Trade,* International Monetary Fund, September 17, 1957. (Mimeographed.)

[33]R. J. Ball and K. Marwah, "The U. S. Demand for Imports, 1948-58," *Review of Economics and Statistics,* November, 1962, pp. 395-401.

[34]M. E. Kreinin, "Effect of Tariff Changes on the Value and Volume of Imports," *op. cit.*

[35]L. B. Krause, "United States Imports and the Tariff," *American Economic Review,* May, 1959.

[36]Textiles have been excluded because imports from Japan had been subject to voluntary export quotas.

[37]Aside from the question of statistical significance, for purposes of the present study the result for the periods 1947-54 and 1947-58 are of primary interest since tariff reductions were concentrated in the 1947-54 period.

[38]The price and tariff elasticities, with their standard errors in parenthesis are as follows:

	Price elasticity		Tariff elasticity	
1947-58	−1.77	(0.32)	−5.64	(2.11)
1947-54	−1.54	(0.31)	−4.49	(1.83)
1954-58	−1.32	(0.21)	−0.52	(0.28)

B. Krause, "United States Imports, 1947-58," *Econometrica,* April, 1962, pp. 221-38.

Kreinin's and Krause's results point to the conclusion that a reduction in tariffs is likely to have a larger effect on imports than an
equivalent change in export prices—a phenomenon which requires
explanation. Aside from the downward bias in least-squares estimates
of price elasticities, it may be that importers regard tariff changes as
permanent and reallocate their purchases accordingly, while changes
in export prices are often considered transitory. Also, a ratchet-effect
could be operative in the second case: Once purchases are accom-
modated to a lower import price, habit formation or simply the
acquired knowledge of foreign goods may limit the shift back to
domestic commodities. On the other hand, we have but few instances
of raising tariffs in the postwar period. Finally, and perhaps·more
importantly, the explanation may lie in the fact that most authors use
changes in nominal tariffs to derive the price change. Because tariff
rates on final products have usually been subject to more drastic
reductions than duties on imported imputs, the effective protective
rates, which govern the volume of imports, were cut by a larger proportion than their nominal counterparts (see formula on p. 33 above).
Thus, observed changes in quantity represent responses to larger
price changes than are superficially apparent. The use of nominal
tariffs in the computations reduces the size of the denominator in the
elasticity equation, and magnifies the elasticity estimates.

Further evidence on the responsiveness of imports to changes in
tariffs is provided in a study by B. A. deVries. DeVries calculated implicit "tariff" elasticities for 176 products on the basis of information
provided by commodity experts regarding the possible long-term
effects on U. S. imports of an assumed reduction—or increase—of the
1939 U. S. tariffs by one-half. For all commodities, taken together,
the weighted average of elasticities is −2.2 for a reduction, and −2.7
for an increase in duties. At the same time, for the three product
groups of the Ball-Marwah study, the following elasticities have been
obtained: crude materials, −1.3; semimanufactures −3.1; and finished
manufactures −3.9.[39] All these pieces of evidence point to the conclusion that the import-demand for manufactures is highly elastic.[40]

[39]B. A. deVries, "Price Elasticities of Demand for Individual Commodities
Imported Into the United States," *International Monetary Fund Staff Papers*,
April, 1951, pp. 397-419.

[40]See also Arnold C. Harberger, "Some Evidence on the International Price
Mechanism," *Journal of Political Economy*, December, 1957, pp. 506-22.

As stated earlier, the Ball and Marwah approach appears the most promising for the problem at hand. But their calculations are based on the years 1948-1958 which include the Korean war and its aftermath. Since these cannot be considered normal years, some of the observations might have been biased, thereby affecting the results improperly. In order to avoid this problem, I have recalculated the elasticity for finished manufactures using quarterly data for 1954-1964 (43 observations). The procedure involved regressing the index of import volume, Y, against real GNP, X, and relative prices, Z, (import price index divided by the corresponding wholesale price index), where all figures are expressed in logarithm. The volume of imports was lagged one quarter behind the two independent variables (income and relative price), and all variables were adjusted for seasonal fluctuations by the use of moving averages. The resulting regression equation is:

$$Y = 4.246 + 2.347\,X - 4.715Z \qquad R = 0.983$$
$$(0.424)\ (0.158)\ \ \ (0.553)$$

It shows an income elasticity of import demand for manufactures of $+2.35$ and a relative price elasticity of -4.7.[41] This figure is consistent with that obtained by adding two standard errors to the Ball and Marwah estimates, as suggested by them (*op. cit.*, Table 3).

Thus, an elasticity estimate was assigned to each of the 85 three-digit SITC commodity groups depending on whether the products contained in it were finished manufactures ($\eta = -4.7$), semi-manufactures ($\eta = -1.38$), or a combination of the two.[42]

It might be objected that applying a uniform elasticity estimate to most commodity groups is an improper procedure. In general, the question whether "aggregated" or "disaggregated" elasticities should be used depends on the problem at hand. Conceptually, the elasticities pertaining to individual commodities are usually computed on the

---

[41]For all commodities, the comparable import-demand equation is:
$$Y = -1.27 + 1.268X - 1.107Z \qquad R = 0.98$$
$$(0.21)(1.178)\ \ \ (0.155)$$

[42]Following is a frequency distribution of the elasticities used:

SITC Section	Number of 3 -or 5-digit groups	Number of Groups with Elasticity of:		
		−4.7	−1.38	Other (in between)
5	12	2	5	5
6	41	29	9	3
7	18	18	0	0
8	14	14	0	0

The conversion from SITC to Schedule A classification was made possible by the conversion table published by the Census Bureau in January, 1963.

assumption that all other prices remain the same. Thus the estimates obtained directly from aggregative data would be lower than a weighted average of the elasticities pertaining to commodity groups (especially if the cross elasticity of demand between the groups is high). In dealing with policies which apply uniformly to all commodities, too much disaggregation should be avoided. At most, disaggregation should be confined to broad categories, between which the cross elasticity of demand is very low. But available data do not permit even such disaggregation in this study.

D. Estimated Increase in U. S. Imports:

Estimates of the increase in American imports as a result of AFTA were made separately for each of the 85 commodity categories in SITC 5-8. If the original tariff rate, expressed as a fraction of the c.i.f. price exclusive of duty, is denoted by t (i.e., a tariff of 100t percent), then under the assumption of constant export prices, U. S. import prices would decline by $\frac{t}{1+t}$[43]. The value of imports (M) will rise by:

$$\Delta M = M \cdot \eta \cdot \frac{t}{1+t}$$

where η is the U. S. import-demand elasticity. Summed over all commodity categories, the estimated increase is $2.8 billion.

For reasons discussed in section B, the assumption that import prices would decline by half the tariff rate is considered closer to reality. The volume of imports would then rise by $\frac{t}{2(1+t)} \cdot \eta$. But foreign export prices would also increase by $t/2$, placing the increase in the value of imports at:

$$\Delta M = M \left[(1 + \frac{1}{2} \cdot \eta \, \frac{t}{1+t}) (1 + \frac{t}{2}) - 1 \right]$$

---

[43]This is the change in price paid by the importer. The price paid by the consumer will decline by a smaller amount, i.e., by:

$$\frac{t}{1+t+m}$$

where m designates the mark-up in the various stages of distribution between the importer and the final consumer. Needless to say, m is likely to be quite sizable, but no information is available about its magnitude. However, since the import-demand elasticities used here apply to the importer rather than the consumer, there is no need to modify the formula used in the text.

or
$$\Delta M = M\frac{t}{2}\left(1 + \frac{\eta}{1+t} + \frac{\eta t}{2(1+t)}\right)$$

Added up over all commodity categories, U. S. imports are estimated to increase by $1.88 billion. The following ten SITC industries, each of which would experience an increase in imports of $60 million or more, account for close to 60 percent of the total increase:

Table 3

SITC Industries Expected to Experience Major Increases in Imports in the Event of AFTA

SITC Number	Industry Description	Estimated Increase in Imports ($ millions)
641	Paper and Paperboard	160.9
653	Other Woven Textile Fabrics	109.9
681 04-08 12, 13	Finished Articles of Iron and Steel	63.1
699	Manufactures of Metal n.e.s.	132.1
721—other than 01	Other Electrical Machinery Apparatus	117.9
732—01	Passenger Road Motor Vehicles	113.6
841	Clothing	138.4
851	Footwear	66.2
864	Watches and Clocks	65.4
899	Manufactured Articles n.e.s.	108.3
	Total	1,075.8

SOURCE: See text.

Although the above estimate will be used in the subsequent analysis, it is interesting to examine the sensitivity of the result to the assumptions made. Under unchanged foreign export prices, and roughly similar (though somewhat smaller) import-demand elasticities, but with tariff rates weighted by the combined imports of the industrial countries (to obtain the aggregate for each SITC group), the estimated increase in U. S. imports would be $1.85 billion (instead of the $2.8 billion mentioned earlier). This lower figure presumably reflects a downward bias imparted by the tariff aggregation procedure under a somewhat similar tariff structure in AFTA countries. On the other hand, if European export prices are assumed to rise by one-third, the estimated increase in American imports is $1.6 billion (again, less then the $1.88 billion mentioned above).

E. IMPORT QUOTAS

As a general rule the United States does not apply quota restrictions to industrial imports. Japan, however, exercises voluntary restrictions on the exports of cotton textiles[44] (imposed in 1957) and 28 other products to the United States. "These are goods the uncontrolled export of which might possibly lead to the establishment of import restrictions in the country of destination." [45] Partly in order to avoid diversion of imports to other sources of supply such as Hong Kong, Taiwan, and India, the bilateral textile agreement between the United States and Japan was replaced in July, 1961, by a short-term arrangement under GATT auspices. It was extended in February, 1962, for a five-year period, as a long-term arrangement designed to regulate international trade in cotton textiles. There is no way of knowing what effect the proposed AFTA would have on this commodity agreement. Neither is it possible to foresee whether the other voluntary export quotas would be dispensed with.[46]

In the present context, we shall attempt a rough estimate of the impact of the Japanese quotas on the U. S. balance of trade. Table 4 shows figures on American imports from Japan; these figures were provided by the Department of Commerce.

Table 4
U. S. Imports From Japan
(*$ million, f.o.b.*)

	Total	Cotton Textiles	28 Other Voluntarily Controlled Products	Total Controlled Products	Total Uncontrolled Products
1957	597	91	128	219	378
1962	1,400	136	252	388	1,012
Change 1957-62	903	45	124	169	634
Percentage Change	151	50	100	77	170

SOURCE: United States Department of Commerce (unpublished).

[44]For some discussion see: *Foreign Trade Policy* Compendium (1958), *op. cit.*, pp. 621-28; United States Tariff Commission, *Cotton Products Report*, Washington, September, 1962; and *Japan Foreign Trade*, Washington, 1958.

[45]United States Department of Commerce, *Overseas Business Reports*, November, 1962, p. 3. The list of commodities includes: plywood, canned and frozen tuna, china dinner sets, sewing machines, certain silk and wool fabrics, bamboo blinds, unglazed mosaic tile, umbrellas and frames, Christmas tree light bulbs, stainless steel flatware, and others.

[46]At the time of writing, it appears that despite pressure by underdeveloped countries for preferential tariff treatment for their industrial exports, the long-term textile agreement would be renewed.

Had the "controlled" items increased by the same percentage as their "noncontrolled" counterparts (170 percent), their imports in 1962 would have been $581 million, i.e., larger by $193 million than the actual $388 million registered. As an approximation, we might assume that the voluntary export controls excluded $193 million of imports from the United States, of which $102 million were cotton textiles.

An imponderable which could not be allowed for is the effect of an AFTA on Japan's exports to Europe. Many Japanese exports are currently barred from West European markets by various means. As these restrictions disappeared, Japan would ship more to Europe, thus lessening her need to export to the United States. On the other hand, she might price some American products out of European markets. The first effect is usually considered stronger than the second, so that on balance this impact would probably be favorable to the United States. However, since there is no way of estimating these effects quantitatively, they were left out of the calculations, as though they would balance each other out in the overall U. S. trade posture.

In total it is estimated that the removal of tariffs and quotas on manufactured products under AFTA would increase American imports by $2,076 million.

F. Industrial Materials

As a further step, we allow for the possibility that AFTA might include nonindustrial commodities: Crude Materials, inedible (SITC Section 2); Minerals, Fuel, Lubricants and Related Materials (SITC Section 3); Animal and Vegetable Oils and Fats (Section 4); and Unwrought Non-ferrous Metals (682.1-689.1). With a few exceptions, tariffs are the main method of protection both here and abroad, and rates tend to be considerably below those applied to industrial products. However, in several instances effective import quotas are currently in use, or were employed in the recent past. The most glaring cases are the U. S. quotas on petroleum, lead, and zinc; and the European and Japanese quotas on coal.

U. S. imports of crude and semimanufactured materials represent approximately one-half of total imports (but they come mainly from non-AFTA countries), and make an important contribution to the supplies of industrial raw materials used in this country. Based on

Ball and Marwah's calculations, each three-digit SITC group was assigned an elasticity figure, depending on whether it contained Crude Materials ($\eta = -0.26$), Crude Foodstuffs ($\eta = -0.34$), Manufactured Foodstuffs ($\eta = -1.87$), or Semimanufactures ($\eta = -1.38$). Since most groups consisted of a combination of two or more categories, an average elasticity, weighted by imports, was assigned to them.[47]

Assuming that import prices would decline by the full amount of the tariff, U. S. imports of materials would rise by $95 million. If, on the other hand, import prices are assumed to decline by half the tariff level, the increase in imports would be $106.7 million.

In 1958, the United States imposed import quotas on lead and zinc.[48] There is one major exporter of these products in the projected AFTA, namely Canada (the rest comes mainly from Latin America). The Department of Commerce estimated that removal of the quotas would raise imports by $45 million. In addition, the United States employed severe quota restrictions on oil imports. The changeover from a liberal to protectionist policy in this field began in 1957 with the institution of semivoluntary restrictions, which became mandatory in 1959. The Petroleum Industry Research Foundation estimates that elimination of these restrictions would raise imports by 1.35 million barrels a day. Valued at an f.o.b. price of $2.25 per barrel, this amounts to approximately $1 billion per year, and is equal to about 16 percent of total domestic production of crude oil and natural gas liquids in 1962. (The amount actually imported in that year was equal to

---

[47]Following are the assigned elasticity estimates:

Old SITC No.	Elasticity	Old SITC No.	Elasticity	Old SITC No.	Elasticity
211	0.26	263	0.45	283	0.26
212	0.26	264	0.26	284	1.04
221	0.28	265	3.50	285	0.71
231	0.26	266	1.38	291	1.12
241	1.38	267	2.50	292	0.37
242	0.42	271	1.22	311, 312, 314	0.26
243	1.38	272-08	0.80	313	1.38
244	1.38	272-06, 07	0.25	411	1.38
251	1.38	272-other	1.26	412, 02-05	0.26
261	0.26	281	0.26	412-other	1.50
262	0.42	282	1.33	413	0.60

[48]See United States Tariff Commission, *Lead and Zinc Report* (Washington, D. C., October, 1960).

nearly 14 percent of domestic production.)[49] However, since the official basis for the restrictions is the National Security Clause of the Trade Expansion Act, they are assumed to remain unaffected by AFTA.

---

[49]These figures were taken from a speech delivered by Mr. John H. Lichtblau, Research Director of the Petroleum Industry Research Foundation, at the London School of Economics in June, 1964. It was made available to me in mimeographed form by Dr. Leslie Grayson of the Cal-Tex Oil Company.

Chapter 4

Effect of an Atlantic Free Trade Area on American Exports

A similar procedure was followed in estimating the expansion of U. S. exports expected to result from an AFTA. That expansion would depend on the tariff rates facing American exports, the elasticity of export supply in the United States, and the elasticity of import demand for manufactures in other industrial countries.

A. Tariff Rates

As in the case of imports, the major source of tariff information was the P.E.P. Report, *Atlantic Tariffs and Trade*. Several adjustments were made in the P.E.P. figures: The German tariff was lowered by 25 percent to conform to the unilateral reductions which took place in August, 1957,[50] and the tariffs of the EEC members were reduced by 10 percent, since their initial 1959 cuts were extended also to third countries. Canada's tariff was adjusted downward by 5 (instead of 10) percent to account for the f.o.b. valuation procedure, because this factor was partly offset when specific duties were converted to their ad valorem equivalents. In addition, the figures had to be supplemented for countries not included in the report: (1) for Japan, Finland, and Greece with data compiled by the Joint Economic Com-

---

[50]P.E.P. Report, *op. cit.*, p. VII.

mittee,[51] supplemented with figures prepared by the Financial Counsellor of the Japanese Embassy for the American Management Association Seminar on Japan; (2) for Spain and Turkey by overall averages supplied by the Department of Commerce.[52]

B. UNITED STATES EXPORT PRICES

In contrast to other industrial countries, exports occupy a very small share of total production in most American industries, making the U. S. export supply elasticity much higher than elsewhere. Moreover, under conditions of relatively high mobility of American resources, coupled with higher levels of unemployment than were prevalent in Europe during the postwar period, a balanced expansion of trade can be carried out without a significant increase in production costs. For these reasons, it will be assumed that the expansion of exports will not necessitate an increase in export prices in the United States. For lack of empirical evidence,[53] this assumption must be made strictly on a priori grounds.

C. IMPORT DEMAND ELASTICITIES

Estimates on import demand elasticities for Western Europe and Japan are few and far between. Calculations prepared in the postwar period showed elasticities around unity in regard to total imports, while higher values obtain if agricultural products are excluded.[54] These estimates are subject to a substantial downward bias, however, and for present purposes more reliance can be placed in the results of recent studies that have examined the effects of changes in duties on imports. With regard to the United Kingdom, M. FG. Scott found that in the 1931-32 period, a 1 percentage point rise in tariffs was accompanied by a fall in the imports of manufactured goods of 4.3 percent.[55] In turn, in a study of the effects of unilateral tariff reduc-

[51]*Trade Restraints in the Western Community*, Washington, 1961. The figures presented there are weighted averages and, as such, are not strictly comparable to the P.E.P. figures.

[52]*Overseas Business Reports.*

[53]A doctoral dissertation in the Graduate School of Business Administration at Michigan State University will investigate this question empirically with respect to the Dillon Round of tariff negotiations.

[54]A. C. Harberger, "Some Evidence on the International Price Mechanism," *Journal of Political Economy*, December, 1957, pp. 506-21.

[55]M. FG. Scott, *A Study of United Kingdom Imports* (Cambridge: University Press, 1962), pp. 168-69.

tions undertaken by Germany in 1956 and 1957, J. Wemelsfelder derived an import demand elasticity of −9.[56]

Although the estimates of Scott and Wemelsfelder indicate the responsiveness of imports to the lowering of tariffs in European countries, they are of limited usefulness for selecting appropriate values of import demand elasticities for the purpose at hand. For one thing, the results are sensitive to conditions of capacity utilization existing in the periods under consideration; for another, figures are not available for all the major countries in Western Europe and for Canada and Japan. Also, the existing estimates do not provide an appropriate commodity breakdown. Consequently, we have derived the elasticity coefficients for these countries from estimates pertaining to the United States. Under the assumption of identical domestic demand and supply[57] elasticities in all areas, the import demand elasticity would be negatively correlated with the share of imports in domestic consumption. Empirical evidence for this a priori relationship, (discussed in Chapter 3), is provided in deVries' study. His study shows that U. S. import demand elasticities average about −2 for commodities in which the ratio of imports to domestic consumption exceeds 27 percent (the average for all 176 products), while the corresponding figure is −3.4 for products where the import-consumption ratio is below the average.[58] Since the share of imports in domestic consumption is considerably smaller in the United States than elsewhere, import demand elasticities are expected to be lower abroad than in the United States.

In previous contributions, the ratio of consumption of import-competing goods to imports has been estimated at 4 for the United States (an import share of 25 percent), 2 for Canada, 3 for the EEC and Japan, 2.6 for the U. K., and 2.2 for Continental EFTA.[59] Ac-

---

[56]J. Wemelsfelder, "The Short-Run Effects of the Lowering of Import Duties in Germany," *Economic Journal*, March, 1960, pp. 94-105.

[57]Considering the level of unemployment and excess capacity in the United States in the past decade, supply elasticities may be higher here than elsewhere. But no adjustments could be made for this factor.

[58]B. A. deVries, "Price Elasticities of Demand for Individual Commodities Imported into the United States," *op. cit.*, p. 413.

[59]For a discussion and elaboration of the procedure and estimates see B. Balassa and M. E. Kreinin: "Trade Liberalization under the Kennedy Round: The Static Effects," *Review of Economics and Statistics*, May 1967; and B. Balassa, "Tariff Protection in Industrial Countries: an Evaluation," *Journal Political Economy*, December 1965, p. 592-93.

cordingly the import-demand elasticities used for these countries in each SITC category, were calculated as the following ratios of the U. S. estimate: Canada, 2/4; EEC and Japan, 3/4; U. K., 2.6/4; and Continental EFTA, 2.2/4.[60]

D. Estimated Increase in U. S. Exports

Estimates were prepared separately for each commodity category and country of destination, on the basis of the formula:

$$\Delta E = E \cdot \eta \frac{t}{1+t}$$

where E is U. S. exports, t is the foreign tariff rate expressed as a fraction of c.i.f. price exclusive of the duty (ad valorem tariff rate is 100t), and η the import-demand elasticity of the AFTA country for the particular SITC commodity group. Added over all commodity categories, the estimated increase in U. S. exports is $1.86 billions. The following five SITC industries, each of which would experience an increase in exports of $100 million or more, account for over one-third of the anticipated total (see Table 5). For the sake of com-

Table 5

SITC Industries Expected to Experience Major Increases in Exports in the Event of AFTA

SITC Number	Industry Description	Estimated Increase in Exports ($ millions)
716-03	Conveying, Hoisting, Excavating, etc. Machinery	98.1
716, other than 03 and 08	Industrial Machinery, n.e.s.	181.3
721, other than 01	Other Electrical Machinery	113.0
732, other than 01 and 03	Other Road Motor Vehicles	116.3
734	Aircraft	144.6
	Total	653.3

SOURCE: See text.

---

[60]The resulting elasticities are fairly consistent with whatever fragmentary evidence is available from other sources on the relation between the U. S. and foreign import-demand elasticities. But such evidence is admittedly very scarce. If anything, these ratios are probably too high, thereby overstating the elasticity of import-demand in foreign countries. The reader who so chooses can adjust the elasticities and the resulting estimates downward.

parison, if instead of unweighted tariffs for each SITC category we use tariffs weighted by the combined imports of industrial countries, the estimated increase in American exports would be $1.62 billion.

E. QUOTAS

In addition to tariffs, American industrial exports are also met by quota barriers. One way to quantify the effect of import quotas is by applying an import demand elasticity to the differential between the world price and the domestic price in the quota-imposing country. However, we have chosen an alternative (more practical) method of relying on the informed judgment of commodity experts. In Japan, significant quota restrictions exist on the importation of 174 industrial products. The Department of Commerce estimates that their removal would increase American industrial exports to that country by $75 to 125 million. In Western Europe there are remnants of quota restrictions on manufacturing imports, and their removal is expected to raise American exports by $15 million. Extensive quantitative restrictions are also in force in both Turkey and Spain. However, since these are imposed mainly for balance of payments considerations rather than for reasons of protection, they are expected to remain unaffected by the projected AFTA (any agreement would have to make special provisions for such cases). It is further assumed that other widespread impediments to U. S. exports, such as the preferences awarded domestic producers by government enterprises in Europe (e.g., the French railways purchasing French diesels), would remain intact. The same applies to the differential rebates on sales taxes of exported commodities practiced by countries in which the sales taxes account for a major share of government revenue.[61] (These factors were also abstracted from in estimating the increase in American imports.)

In sum, the effect of quota removal on American exports is estimated at $115 million.

---

[61]This question is a bone of contention in the Kennedy Round. The practice discriminates against American exporters who receive no such rebate because the United States relies mainly on the income tax for federal revenue (see *Trade Talk*, CNTP, Washington, July 23, 1964). The problem is one reason for the need to harmonize taxes in the EEC. (For a recent report, see the Amsterdamsche Bank, *Economic Quarterly Review*, June, 1964, pp. 38-41). See also R. Z. Aliber and H. Stein, "The Price of U. S. Exports and the Mix of U. S. Direct and Indirect Taxes," *American Economic Review*, September, 1964, pp. 703-10.

F. Nonagricultural Materials

American exports of materials in 1960 amounted to $3 billion. They encountered an average tariff of 4.05 percent.[62] The same elasticity estimate was assumed for each SITC group as in the case of imports. Under the assumption of infinite supply elasticity in the United States, the elimination of tariffs would increase export by $67 million.

In addition, Western Europe and Japan maintain tight restrictions on coal imports. A 1963 Report by Robert Nathan and Associates, commissioned by the United States Department of the Interior, estimated that by 1970 the United States could increase its coal exports by $300-700 million over 1962. Of this figure, about 90 percent would be destined to AFTA countries. It is of interest that most, if not all, of this coal would be mined in the depressed areas of West Virginia and central Pennsylvania. However, we shall assume that these quotas would not be removed as a result of AFTA.

G. Elimination of Discrimination By Europe's Regional Groups

A major benefit to the United States from the establishment of AFTA would be the elimination of discrimination by the European Economic Community (EEC) and the European Free Trade Area Association (EFTA). In assessing the magnitude of this gain, our estimate is confined to the static diversion of trade. There is no need to balance it against the dynamic gains to American exports from European integration. Such gains, which arise from the faster growth rate within the EEC and EFTA, would presumably be fully realized by the time an AFTA is set up; and the elimination of the discrimination would not affect them.

One reason for basing this study on 1960 trade data is that they were virtually unaffected by discriminatory practices. The first intra-EEC tariff cut of 10 percent, in January, 1959, was generally applied to nonmember countries, and no discrimination against outsiders existed until mid-1960 when the second internal reduction took place. The first move by the EEC nations toward aligning their individual external tariff with the future common external tariff was taken in January 1, 1961, and the Dillon Round of tariff negotiations helped

---

[62]Unweighted average for each country, but weighted for all countries by their GNP.

minimize the discrimination against outsiders in the early 1960's. This indeed was one of the avowed purposes of the 1958 extension of the Trade Agreements Act. The degree of Common Market discrimination was generally between 10 and 20 percent in 1961.

This situation changed radically toward the mid-1960's, as the steps in the integration process were being taken at an accelerated pace. It is reasonable to assume that a complete customs union for industrial products will be achieved by the Six before the end of the decade. Likewise, the seven members of EFTA will complete the formation of a free trade area by that time. Presumably, U. S. exports will experience the full diversionary impact toward the end of the 1960's; and removal of the discrimination with the creation of an AFTA would result in a comparable benefit.

Since the late 1950's an abundant literature has appeared regarding the effect of the EEC on nonmember countries.[63] Most recently, the Brookings Report[64] presented a quantitative estimate of the diversionary impact on American exports. For each of 61 U. S. industrial exports to the Common Market, the authors calculated the additional protection afforded by the common external tariff to the low-cost producers[65] within the Community. Then, applying a uniform elasticity of -2, they arrived at a figure of $200 million as the loss to American industrial exports caused by the EEC.

I have two reservations concerning this result. First, the method employed in deriving it implicitly assumes a very high elasticity of supply by the low-cost producers in the community, enabling them to increase their domination of the market (under the tariff protection) without increasing prices. To the extent that the EEC members are operating at capacity, and even suffer from shortages of capacity, this could not be the case. At the very least, the discriminatory tariff may cause them to divert some of their exports from external to in-

[63]See for example the papers by Erik Thorbecker, Bela Balassa, and L. B. Krause on "Problems of Regional Integration," *American Economic Review (Proceedings)*, May, 1963, pp. 147-96. For a summary of studies on the trade creation effect of the EEC see J.H.F. Schilderinck and R. A. Van Straelen, "Attempts Toward a Quantitative Analysis of the Influence of European Integration on the Benelux Economy" in *The Market Economy and Western European Integration*, Seventh Flemish Economic Congress, Louvain, Belgium, May, 1965.

[64]Salant, *et al., The United States Balance of Payments in 1968, op. cit.,* Chapter IV.

[65]For a list of the 22 leading commodity groups, see *ibid.,* p. 103.

ternal destinations. That would relieve some competitive pressure against American exports in third markets, and perhaps even cause some reduction in the EEC exports to the United States.

The Brookings Report denies the probability of such export retardation. It presumes that the expansion of output would often result in economies of scale, and that: "In an industrially advanced country, output usually can be increased; the door is rarely slammed in the face of willing customers" (p. 113). But the door need not be "slammed" for exports to be retarded. The effect would usually take the form of longer waiting periods for European products and less aggressive sales efforts outside the Community on the part of European producers. These are highly probable results for an inflation-ridden economy, and the Brookings Report itself alludes to them in a different context (p. 100). The statistics used by the Brookings group support the position that no retardation has taken place relate to 1961. But in that year there was still no significant discrimination against outsiders. A priori, the persistent pressure against capacity, despite the continuing increase in efficiency, would lead to at least some increase in imports and retardation of exports. This is particularly true in this case of trade diversion leading to an *unbalanced* expansion in the exports of members of the EEC.

In order to account for this factor, we assume that one-half of the European price advantage imparted through the EEC discrimination would be wiped out by domestic price increases.[66]

On the other hand, it is highly probable that the elasticity figure of -2 is too low. Specifically, the Brookings technique shows the volume of U. S. exports excluded from the Community markets as a result of a decline in the price of exports of a competitor within the Community. To the extent that the change in relative prices applies to the national market of the competitor (because the Common External Tariff differs from the original national tariff), the elasticity of demand for American exports is the relevant figure. But the country's own tariff may move in either direction. Since most of the price differentials would occur in other Community markets, the relevant figure is the elasticity of substitution between American and European manufactured products. This figure has been estimated at 2.5 for

---

[66]This is probably a minimum price increase. In order to distinguish this case from the balanced expansion of trade, it may even be plausible to assume a price increase of two-thirds, yielding a discrimination to only one-third of price.

the interwar period.[67] But as in the case of import-demand elasticities, much higher estimates were obtained for the postwar period.

Most recently H. B. Junz and R. R. Rhomberg[68] obtained substitution elasticities for industrial products ranging all the way from −2 to −12. They also estimated the elasticity of demand for exports at −3.3 and −5.5 for periods of six and ten years, respectively. Based on their work, I assumed a substitution elasticity of −3.5—a figure consistent with the import-demand elasticities employed in this study. It is also consistent with my own estimate of −2.6 for the short-run (three-year period) elasticity of substitution. Appendix II-B explains the method by which the latter figure was obtained.

In order to estimate the diversionary impact on U. S. exports to the EEC, we selected the 26 three- and five-digit SITC categories in the industrial section, in which U. S. exports to the Community in 1960 exceeded $10 million. The selected items cover 91 percent of U. S. industrial exports to the EEC. Half the level of the common external tariff, t, was regarded as the measure of discrimination. For each selected industry, the diversionary impact was estimated according to the following formula:

$$\Delta E_{U.S.} = \frac{1}{2} \cdot \frac{t}{t+t} \cdot 3\frac{1}{2} \cdot E_{U.S.}$$

where $E_{U.S.}$ denotes U. S. exports to the EEC in 1960. However, a minor adjustment had to be made in some instances. For most commodities the common external tariff is an unweighted average of the tariff rates of the four constituent customs areas. For the most part, this involved an increase in the tariffs of Germany and Benelux, and a reduction in those of Italy and France. Inasmuch as U. S. exports to the EEC are not equally distributed among the four areas, the average tariff facing them may either increase or decline as a result of the adjustment to the common level. This factor was accounted for by the use of import-demand elasticities, and the results added to those obtained from the above formula.

Added up for all industries, the estimated diversionary effect of the EEC amounts to $300 million. The main industries so affected are shown in Table 6.

---

[67]Arnold Harberger, *op. cit., The Journal of Political Economy,* December, 1957, p. 516, Table 3.

[68]H. B. Junz and R. R. Rhomberg, "Prices and Export Performance of Industrial Countries, 1953-1963," *IMF Staff Papers,* July, 1965, pp. 244-71.

Table 6

SITC Industries Sustaining Main Discriminatory Effect of the EEC

SITC Number	Industry Description	Estimated Diversion ($ millions)
512	Organic Chemicals	$ 30
599	Miscellaneous Chemicals	30
714	Office Machinery	12
715	Metal Working Machinery	14
716	Industrial Machinery, n.e.s.	42
721	Electrical Machinery	20
732	Road Motor Vehicles	19
734	Aircraft	46
	Total	$213

SOURCE: See text.

In the field of nonagricultural crude materials, which comprises 22 percent of U. S. exports to the EEC, the Common External Tariff tends to be low or zero, and the amount of diversion was not estimated.[69] Finally, the EEC members would discriminate in favor of their Associated African territories (mainly the French) and against Latin American countries which are the traditional customers of the United States, depriving the latter nations of foreign exchange with which to finance imports. This indirect cost to American exports is also excluded because there is no way of quantifying it.[70]

A similar procedure was followed in estimating the diversionary effect of EFTA, except that in the absence of a common external tariff, the degree of discrimination against outsiders varies from one member to another. In 1960, there were 25 three- and five-digit SITC industries within the industrial sector in which U. S. exports to EFTA exceeded $10 million; they accounted for 88 percent of total U. S. industrial exports to EFTA. In two of these industries (673 and 689) the United States faces virtually no competition within EFTA, and the degree of discrimination is assumed to be nil. In nine industries,

---

[69]The Brookings Report (*op. cit.*, pp. 105-106) estimates a diversionary loss of $100 millions in aluminum, certain petroleum products, and other items. But it is not clear how this figure is arrived at. That Report also estimates a $350 million loss to U. S. exports of agricultural products, which do not concern us here.

[70]The Brookings Report, *op. cit.*, pp. 111-12, estimates this cost at $100 million, but does not indicate how the figure was arrived at.

there is one major competitor; in fifteen industries, two major competitors; and in two industries, three main competitors. The United Kingdom occupies a predominant position in almost all industries. It appears as the first or (sometimes) the second major competitor in 21 of the 23 industries. Consequently, in a large measure EFTA would involve discrimination against American exports competing with similar British products. Because of the existence of excess industrial capacity in Great Britain, its supply elasticity is probably higher than that of the EEC. Nevertheless, we shall assume, as before, that half of the tariff reduction would be consumed in price increases.

Since EFTA does not call for a common external tariff, and only involves the elimination of duties on the intra-area trade, the degree of discrimination against outsiders can be measured for each industry and in each country by its external duty. The same formula was employed as in the case of the EEC. However, in industries 533, 734, and 862, the U. K. is the only intra-EFTA exporter. That means that in the British market itself there would be no discrimination against American exports as a result of EFTA.

Summing up the results for all countries and for the products involved, we obtained $150 million as the static measure of discrimination by EFTA against the United States in the manufacturing sector. The main industries affected are shown in Table 7.

Table 7

SITC Industries Sustaining Main Discriminatory Effect of EFTA

SITC Number	Industry Description	Estimated Diversion ($ millions)
512	Organic Chemicals	$10
599	Miscellaneous Chemicals	13
681	Iron and Steel	17
715	Metal Working Machinery	14
716	Industrial Machinery, n.e.s.	28
721	Electrical Machinery	12
732	Road Motor Vehicles	13
	Total	$107

SOURCE: See text.

EFTA countries' tariffs on nonagricultural raw materials tend to be zero or very low. It is practically impossible to find a product which would meet the conditions for significant diversion, namely, moderate (to high) tariff, sizable imports from the United States, and EFTA-U. S. competition within an EFTA market. The amount of diversion was therefore assumed to be nil.

The above estimates abstract from the probable improvement of the terms of trade of the integrating blocs at the expense of outsiders, including the United States. On the other hand, there might be some retardation of other European exports to the United States, as the demand for them rises within the blocs. That possibility was also excluded from the calculations.

In total, we estimate that the elimination of European discrimination under AFTA would yield a gain to U. S. exports of $450 million.

Chapter 5

Summary — Effect of an Atlantic Free Trade Area on U.S. Trade

An Atlantic Free Trade Area involving the removal of tariffs and quotas on nonagricultural products would affect the volume of the

Table 8
Estimated Changes in U. S. Nonagricultural Trade
Under AFTA
($ millions)

Source of Change	Imports	Exports
Elimination of Tariffs on Industrial Products	1,883	1,856
Elimination of Quotas on Industrial Products	193	115
Elimination of Tariffs and Quotas on Materials	107	67
Elimination of European Discrimination		450
Total	2,183	2,488

SOURCE: See text.

U. S. foreign trade as shown in Table 8. American merchandise exports in 1960 amounted to $17.5 billion, placing the projected increase at 14 percent of the total. Merchandise imports in the same year were over $14.5 billion, and the anticipated increase of $2.18 billion constitutes 15 percent of the total. AFTA would have a net favorable effect on the U. S. trade balance to the tune of $0.3 billion; namely, less than 10 percent of the 1960 surplus on merchandise trade. Over the long run, the balance of payments would improve further as a result of the anticipated favorable effect on the capital account (see below, Part III).

One element totally absent from the analysis thus far is the feedback effect. This effect concerns the nonreserves accumulating countries, whose imports depend on the availability of foreign exchange over a given period. Thus, with a rise and fall in their exports, one may anticipate that their imports will follow suit, a circumstance which applies primarily to the developing nations. Most European countries are not in this category, and indeed the Brookings Report assigns to them a zero feedback ratio. Of the countries included in the projected AFTA, only Japan and Canada are assigned positive ratios of 0.5 and 0.7, respectively, after the fourth round of spending.[71] These figures reflect the fact that the two countries are good customers of the United States, and that a substantial proportion of any net increase in their dollar earnings is spent in this country. Thus, if an AFTA would affect favorably (unfavorably) their balance of payments, there would be an indirect favorable (unfavorable) effect on the American balance of payments. This effect was not incorporated into our calculations because of the questionable validity of the two large feedback ratios. Japan and Canada may well attempt to accumulate reserves as they have done in the past. Japan was one of only four nonreserve currency nations which accumulated over $1 billion in reserves during the 1958-1962 period.[72] For this reason, the omission of the feedback effect is not likely to impart a serious bias to the estimates.

Another important omission is that of the dynamic effects. The estimates presented thus far are all static in nature. They are concerned with the direct relation between the removal of barriers to trade and the increase in the volume of trade. In other words, they focus on the reallocation of resources from import-competing to export industries under the assumption of unchanged technology and other conditions of production. But the nonreversible dismantling of tariff and quota restrictions has other far reaching effects in changing the conditions of production and distribution, because it *increases the size of the market*.[73] Ever since Adam Smith, economists have realized that the degree of specialization is determined by the size of the market. Thus, when the vast region of AFTA replaces the national

[71]See the Brookings Report on the U. S. Balance of Payments, *op. cit.*, p. 276; and the shortcomings of their estimates outlined on p. 277.

[72]See my paper in the Joint Economic Committee *Compendium on the U. S. Balance of Payments*, Washington, 1963, pp. 260-61.

[73]For a detailed discussion see H. Liebenstein, "Allocative Efficiency vs. X-Efficiency," *American Economic Review*, June 1966, pp. 392-415; and Bela Balassa, *The Theory of Economic Integration* (Homewood, Ill., R. D. Irwin, 1961).

boundaries as the area within which commodities can move freely, some basic transformations can be expected to occur in the constituent economies.

It is immediately apparent that both inter- and intra-industry specialization would be enhanced, and economies of scale would be realized on both the plant and firm level. This would make possible better organization of production, and bring about improvements in the methods of production. The attendant increase in the size of firms is likely to be accompanied by intensified (rather than reduced) competition because a large market can support many sizable firms. Larger expenditures on research and development could then be supported, and the rise in the competitive spirit would spur such expenditures, thereby raising the level of technology. Technological skill would spread across national boundaries via foreign investments and other means.

Unfortunately, these and other dynamic influences cannot be readily incorporated into theoretical models. Neither can they be quantified in the same manner as the static effects. But there is abundant empirical evidence concerning their importance; evidence which suggests a strong positive correlation between market size and growth rate. Indeed many economists consider them far more important then the static effects. The discussion may be concluded with a quotation from a recent article dealing with this subject:

One idea that emerges from this study is that firms and economies do not operate on an outer-bound production possibility surface consistent with their resources. Rather they actually work on a production surface that is well within that outerbound. This means that for a variety of reasons people and organization normally work neither as hard nor as effectively as they could. In situations where competitive pressure is light, many people will trade the disutility of greater effort, of search and the control of other peoples' activities, for the utility of feeling less pressure and of better interpersonal relations. But in situations where competitive pressures are high, and hence the costs of such trades are also high, they will exchange less of the disutility of effort for the utility of freedom from pressure, etc. Two general types of movements are possible. One is along a production surface towards greater allocative efficiency and the other is from a lower surface to a higher one that involves greater degrees of X-efficiency. The data suggest that in a great many instances the amount to be gained by increasing allocative efficiency is trivial while the amount to be gained by increasing X-efficiency is frequently significant.[74]

[74]H. Liebenstein "Allocative Efficiency vs. X-Efficiency," *American Economic Review,* June, 1966, p. 413.

Not all countries will enjoy identical dynamic benefits from AFTA. Other things being equal, the smaller the constituent country, the larger the gain it is likely to reap from integration. Presumably a country the size of the United States can enjoy many of these benefits without any integration. But even here the consumer would gain from intensified foreign competition in steel and other oligopolistic industries. With respect to the large European countries, informed opinion is divided on the extent to which their individual markets can support large scale *and* competitive firms. But there is little doubt that the greatest contribution would be made to the growth rates of the small European countries and Canada. And as their incomes rise so will their imports; in particular they can be expected to increase their imports of sophisticated industrial products which have high income elasticity of demand and in which the United States tends to specialize. Therefore, the dynamic factors are likely to exert a strong favorable influence on the American trade balance in the long run.

Chapter 6

Effect of Alternative Arrangements on the U. S. Balance of Trade

We proceed now to compare the anticipated effects of AFTA on the U. S. trade balance with the impact of three alternative policies. The effect of these arrangements will be estimated on the basis of the same assumptions used in studying AFTA, making it unnecessary to repeat the discussion of tariffs, elasticities, and other factors.

A. EUROPE'S REGIONAL GROUPS

As the first alternative to AFTA, we consider the continuation and completion of the current integration trends in Europe. Both the European Economic Community (EEC) and the European Free Trade Area Association (EFTA), discriminate against American exports and exert an unfavorable influence on the U. S. balance of trade. The static effect of trade diversion was estimated in Chapter 4 at $450 million.[75] As such, the situation now emerging in Europe is distinctly inferior to AFTA from the point of view of the U. S. balance of trade. It is needless to emphasize that much more than this narrow criterion is involved.

[75]On the basis of 1952 figures, Tibor Scitovsky (*Economic Theory and Western European Integration*, Stanford, 1958) estimated that a customs union comprising the Six, the United Kingdom, and the Scandinavian countries, would cause a loss to the rest of the world of $540 million, out of total exports of $10 billion. This loss would consist of trade diversion and deterioration of the outsiders' terms of trade.

However, when European integration is considered as an alternative to AFTA, rather than as part of it, the diversionary effect must be modified in two directions by unknown amounts, to allow for dynamic factors. First, it ought to be increased by the amount of "investment diversion"; [76] i.e., the U. S. investment capital attracted to Europe because of the trade discrimination (for some discussion see Part III, below). Second, it should be offset by the increase in U. S. exports resulting from the internal dynamic growth effect in the integrated areas. The latter impact is impossible to measure in practice primarily because the magnitude of the internal growth effect is unpredictable.

Having outlined the factors involved in these estimates, we can consider the possibility of a merger between the two European blocs. From the point of view of their external trade relations, Britain and some of the EFTA countries have a strong inducement to join the EEC. This accounts, at least in part, for the recurrent British attempts to enter the Common Market, as well as for the intentions of Austria and Denmark to negotiate either associate or full membership. But the obstacles to a bridge between the two blocs are great. The differences in the domestic agricultural policies, the traditional overseas ties of the U. K., and the general political attitude of the French leadership militates against a full measure of success in the near future. And in the long run Britain may opt for a closer association with the United States (see alternative, section B) than with Europe.

Considering all the difficulties involved, it is impossible to speculate on the conditions surrounding a possible merger between the two trade groupings. But it is almost certain that such a merger would result in a lower degree of economic and political cohesion than that of the EEC.

By the same token, there are too many imponderables to permit an estimate of the effect of such an arrangement on American exports. Neither the nature of the arrangement nor its effect on such crucial variables as the external tariff are known. Most probably, the diversionary effect would be larger than that of the combined EEC and EFTA ($450 million.) This is so because a wider range of American products would be excluded from a wider area by the low cost European suppliers. On the other hand, it is possible that if Britain

---

[76]See M. E. Kreinin, "On the Dynamic Effects of Customs Unions," *Journal of Political Economy,* April, 1964.

and Scandinavia joined the EEC in a customs union, they would exert a downward pressure on the external tariff.

B. AFTA WITHOUT THE EEC

Political pressures as well as economic considerations may preclude the establishment of either a European-wide or an Atlantic-wide free trade area. In that event, the United States may find it advisable to encourage and even sponsor an industrial free trade area encompassing the non-EEC nations in the Atlantic community.[77] At the very least, the arrangement would give the participating countries considerable compensation for being barred from the EEC.

U. S. industrial imports from the area encompassed by this arrangement approximated $3.4 billion in 1960, while her exports to the group exceeded $4.4 billion. Using the same disaggregative approach as in the case of AFTA (and similar assumptions), we estimate an increase of $1,356 million in U. S. imports and of $1,275 million in U. S. exports. To these two figures, respectively, we must add $193 million and $112 million[78]—the results of quota removal—while U. S. exports will benefit by a further $150 million as EFTA discrimination is removed. We obtain the following totals: additional U. S. imports: $1,549 million; additional U. S. exports: $1,537 million.

But AFTA without the EEC would also involve trade discrimination on both sides. The EEC would discriminate against the United States causing a loss of $300 million in exports. (Note, however, that

---

[77]It should be noted that the EEC would be under considerable economic pressure to join AFTA. Apart from the discriminatory impact on trade exerted by a wide area which includes North America, the attainment of an integrated and powerful capital market would be impeded if the Six remainded aloof. Observe, for example, the following report of the deliberations by the Federation of National Banking Associations of the EEC:

"The bankers agreed that further significant progress in monetary integration within the EEC is far distant unless new political initiatives are undertaken to that end. They stated that such progress to date has been slight . . . . It was thought unlikely that integration of capital markets within Europe would be truly achieved while Europe's two leading financial centers, London and Zurich, were excluded; yet neither the United Kingdom nor Switzerland were members of the EEC.

"The same type of problem arises again in the field of export credits and export credit insurance, which the Federation has examined at length. Harmonization of such facilities would be meaningful only if it included the United Kingdom, the United States, and Japan." IMF, *International Financial News Survey*, June 26, 1964, p. 206.

[78]Only $3 million of the quota restrictions are allocated to EEC countries.

this discrimination would take place in any event.) On the other hand, American exports would benefit from discrimination against the EEC in other AFTA countries. To estimate the magnitude of this benefit, I selected fifty SITC industries in which the United States and the EEC compete in the markets of Japan, Canada, and "other Europe." The tariff rates levied by third countries on each article would constitute the measure of discrimination against the EEC. Given the high elasticity of supply in the United States, it can be assumed that no increase in export prices would take place. Thus by multiplying the common elasticity of substitution by the degree of discrimination on each manufactured article in the non-EEC countries, we obtained the percentage reduction in EEC exports resulting from the discrimination. These percentages were then applied to the 1960 EEC export figures to each country, to derive dollar estimates of their prospective decline. The decline in each case is equal to the export gain of the non-EEC countries, part of which would accrue to the United States. The allocation of that part was based on the share of U. S. exports in the total exports of the gaining countries (all trade data pertaining to 1960), and the assignment was made separately for each product and country. The gain amounted to $0.7 billion, with various machinery items accounting for over 40 percent of the total. Thus AFTA without the EEC would raise American exports by $1.9 billion,[79] and American imports by $1.5 billion, yielding an increase in the trade surplus of $0.4 billion.

We can only speculate on the prospective changes in the U. S. foreign investments account. On the basis of the survey discussed in Part III, this account is likely to experience a favorable shift, primarily as a result of curtailed investments in Canada. But since discrimination by the EEC would continue to attract American capital, the improvement may be smaller than under AFTA. The overall effect on the U. S. balance of payments is therefore likely to be favorable; and judged solely by this criterion, an AFTA without the EEC may be somewhat more desirable then an all-inclusive AFTA.

C. Tariff Reduction Under the Most Favored Nation Clause

As a final alternative, we consider the effect of successive rounds of GATT's negotiations on the U. S. balance of trade. At the time

[79]$1,537 m. − $300 m. + $700 m.

of writing the Kennedy Round of negotiations is clouded with problems, and its outcome is far from certain. The 50 percent across the board cut was abandoned for all practical purposes as a realistic expectation, and the number of exceptions to any general tariff reduction is likely to be significant. It is therefore difficult to select a working hypothesis for the purpose of assessing the effects on U. S. trade. For lack of a better alternative, we shall assume as a first approximation that the original expectation of 50 percent linear cut would eventually be realized (probably not at the present Round but in subsequent sessions), recognizing that this is merely a benchmark.

In estimating the effect of this arrangement on U. S. trade we shall treat separately the AFTA and non-AFTA members of GATT. For the first group, the 50 percent reduction in tariffs is anticipated to take place on a reciprocal basis. Their effect on American trade would amount to one-half of that estimated in Chapter V for the complete elimination of tariffs. Likewise, the degree of EEC and EFTA discrimination against the United States would be halved. If it is further assumed that import quotas would not be affected, exports would rise by $1.2 billion, while imports would increase by $1.0 billion.

On the other hand, most of the non-AFTA GATT members are underdeveloped countries, which would be unable to offer reciprocal concessions. Since many of them are beset by balance of payments problems, they could not permit the linear tariff reduction to have a full impact on their imports. They would either introduce smaller cuts, or resort to other means of restricting their imports. In many cases, the permitted increase in imports would be governed by the rise in export earnings. Furthermore, one of the demands voiced by underdeveloped countries at the 1964 Geneva Conference on Trade and Development was for freer access to the markets of industrial nations (mainly through preferential tariff treatment) on a nonreciprocal basis. Since that demand was met by a favorable response from the developed countries, it is reasonable to expect that no reciprocal concessions would be forthcoming.

A 50 percent linear cut in duties on their nonagricultural exports is estimated to increase U. S. imports by $157 millions. However, total exports of underdeveloped countries to all members of AFTA (including the effect of reduced European discrimination) would rise by $292 million. Under the assumption that nonindustrial countries spend all increases in their foreign exchange earnings, i.e., they do not accumulate reserves, their increased sales would provide a feedback in the form of higher imports from the industrial countries. Ultimately, about 95 percent of the foreign exchange spent in less developed areas would return to the industrial economies. Based on the pattern of world trade in 1960, the share of the United States in this feedback is estimated at $118 million.[80]

In total, the estimated increase in U. S. exports is put at $1.3 billion, and that of imports at $1.15 billion, yielding a $150 million improvement in the balance of trade.

D. Summary and Comparison

We are now in position to compare the "static" effect of four alternative trade arrangements on the U. S. balance of trade (see Table 9).

Table 9

Effect of Alternative Trade Arrangements on United States External Trade

($ millions)

Trade Arrangement	Imports	Change in U.S. Exports	Trade Balance
(a) AFTA	+2,188	+2,488	+300
(b) European Integration		− 450	−450
(c) AFTA without the EEC	+1,500	+1,900	+400
(d) 50 Percent M.F.N. Tariff Reduction	+1,150	+1,300	+150

SOURCE: See text.

Three of the possible arrangements would have a favorable effect on the U. S. external trade balance. But the figures do not embody any dynamic factors which might come into play in some or all of the trade arrangements. It goes without saying that there are other more important considerations which have bearing on the relative desirability of these policies. Consider, for example, the choice between alternatives (a) and (c). The latter policy would be somewhat more beneficial to the U. S. trade balance than the first. However, AFTA without the EEC may have severe political implications, since it would deepen the split in the Atlantic Alliance. On the other hand, in the

---

[80]See B. Balassa and M. E. Kreinin "Trade Liberalization Under the Kennedy Round—The Static Effects," *Review of Economics and Statistics,* May, 1967.

international financial arena, such an arrangement could result in two large currency blocs—one using the dollar as its main reserve currency, and the other employing some composite EEC unit which may eventually evolve. This would permit the establishment of fixed exchange rates within each bloc (provided that the constituent countries reach some measure of financial integration, or at least close coordination of policies), and fluctuating rates between the two blocs, thereby alleviating the increasingly pressing problem of international liquidity. A full discussion of these considerations is beyond the scope of this volume. They are mentioned only as a reminder that the effect of a certain policy on the U. S. external trade position is not the paramount factor in determining its desirability.

Appendix II

U. S. Imports of Merchandise—Free and Dutiable

Total Imports
($ billions)

Year or Yearly Average	Total	Free	Dutiable	Percent Free	Calculated Duties	Ratio of Duty to: Total Imports (In Percent)	Ratio of Duty to: Dutiable Imports (In Percent)
1926-1930	4.0	2.6	1.4	65.8	0.6	13.7	40.0
1931-1935	1.7	1.1	0.6	63.1	0.3	18.5	50.0
1946-1950	6.6	3.8	2.7	58.4	0.4	6.7	16.0
1951-1955	10.8	6.0	4.8	55.4	0.6	5.4	12.0
1956-1960	13.6	5.8	7.7	43.1	0.9	6.5	11.4
1960	14.7	5.8	8.9	39.5	1.1	7.4	5.9
1961	14.4	5.6	8.7	38.1	1.1	7.4	5.7

Percent of Free Imports
by Economic Classes

	Crude Materials	Crude Foodstuffs	Manufactured Foodstuffs	Semi-manufactures	Finished Manufactures
1926-1930	82.8	80.4	18.5	71.3	39.0
1931-1935	77.4	83.2	30.6	68.2	44.5
1946-1950	63.4	83.4	15.6	55.9	52.3
1951-1955	59.7	87.2	14.1	51.7	44.1
1956-1960	54.4	85.7	2.2	40.9	30.9
1960	55.9	84.7	2.0	37.4	27.6
1961	52.9	83.6	2.1	36.7	29.3

SOURCE: Bureau of the Census, *Statistical Abstract of the United States: 1962*, pp. 890, 892.

APPENDIX II-B

A METHOD FOR ESTIMATING ELASTICITIES OF DEMAND FOR A COUNTRY'S EXPORTS, AND ELASTICITIES OF SUBSTITUTION IN INTERNATIONAL TRADE

For each industrial country the U.N. publication *Monthly Bulletin of Statistics* provides export unit-value and volume indexes for manufactured products, while the publication *Commodity Trade Statistics* (also by the United Nations) furnishes quarterly and annual data on the value of exports by SITC commodity groups and by country of destination.

From the first source, construct an index of change, over time, of each country's competitive position abroad. This is a ratio of the country's export price index, divided by a weighted average of the price indexes of the competing countries. The value or volume of exports can be used as weights in computing the denominator. This ratio constitutes the price component of the elasticity formula. Note that unlike in the case of import-demand elasticities, "relative price" here is a ratio of two export prices; domestic prices do not appear in the denominator of the relative price component.

Next, from the second source obtain for each industrial country a time series of the value of its manufacturing exports. Between any two points of time, each country either lost or gained in its share of world exports—the "world" consisting of a matrix of the countries under consideration. Assuming that no significant changes occurred in supply conditions, the change in each country's share can be attributed mainly to price and income effects. The income effect depends on the income elasticity of demand in each importing country. Had that elasticity been the same with respect to every commodity group, and had income changes been the same in all importing countries, there would have been no need to account for the income effect. This however is unlikely to be the case. Since exporting countries tend to specialize in their exports and also tend to have traditional markets, the differential impact of income change will be manifested mainly in the commodity composition and geographical distribution of each country's exports. These effects need to be removed.

Following Lamfalussy,[81] denote the country's exports in the year under consideration by X', her base year exports by X, and the per-

---

[81]See: A. Lamfalussy, *The United Kingdom and the Six* (Homewood: Richard D. Irwin, 1963), Appendix I to chapter V, pp. 137-40.

centage change in world exports between the two years by r. Then
the country's gain $(+)$ or loss $(-)$ is represented by:

(a) $X' - rX$.

This total change can now be broken into three components, as follows: The effect of *market distribution* is the difference between what
the country's exports would have been had it maintained its base-
period share in each market, and what it would have been, had it
maintained its overall share in the world. It is represented by:

(b) $\Sigma r_i X_i - rX$.

Where r_i is the percentage increase in the exports of all industrial
countries to market i, and X_i is the base year exports of the country
under consideration to market i.

Next, the effect of shifts in *commodity composition* is the difference between what the country's exports would have been had it
maintained its base period share in each commodity and every market,
and what its exports would have been had it maintained its share in
every market. It is represented by the formula:

(c) $\Sigma r_{ij} X_{ij} - \Sigma r_i X_i$.

Where r_{ij} is the percentage change in world exports of commodity j
to market i, and X_{ij} is the base year exports of commodity j to market i
by the country under consideration. Steps b and c are interchangeable.

Finally, the effect of changes in the country's *competitive position*
is:

(d) $X' - \Sigma r_{ij} X_{ij}$.

Formulas (b-d) add up to formula (a).

The change in each country's competitive position is then deflated by its export unit-value index for manufacturing with the result
showing the change in the volume of exports. Thus, the method yields
for each country a time series for relative export prices, and a corresponding series for changes in the volume of exports attributed
to variations in its competitive position. When both variables are
expressed in percentage terms, a simple regression of quantity against
price would yield the elasticity of demand for the country's exports.[82]

Elasticities of substitution can be computed by a variant of the
same technique. Here we wish to establish a relationship between

---

[82]A. Ph.D. dissertation, now in progress at the Graduate School of Business
Administration, Michigan State University, will construct such estimates for two-
digit SITC commodity groups for each of ten industrial countries.

changes in a country's competitive position in a given market and the change in the volume of its exports to that market attributable to the relative price change. The change in the competitive position of country X in market Y is a ratio of X's own export price index to the price index of its competitors. The latter index is computed as a weighted average of the export price indexes of the other competing countries, using each country's exports to market Y as weights. The difference between the resulting ratio and 100 yields the percentage change (from the base year) in price competitiveness of country X in market Y.

Corresponding to the relative price index, we compute the share of each exporting country in each of the markets by removing the effect of commodity composition. Essentially, this is the difference between actual exports of country X to market Y, and what that export would have been had X maintained its base year share in each three-digit SITC commodity group, the resulting dollar figure being deflated by the exporter's unit value index. When the price and the associated volume changes are expressed in percentage terms, a regression between them would yield the elasticity of substitution. Using a matrix of 10 by 10 industrial countries, and confining the analysis to changes between 1955 and 1957, that elasticity was estimated at −2.6 for manufactured products.[83]

---

[83]For further discussion of this method, see M. E. Kreinin, "Price Elasticities in International Trade," *The Review of Economics and Statistics* (forthcoming).

Part **III**

Effect of an Atlantic Free Trade on the U.S. Foreign Investment Account

PART III

Effect of an Atlantic Free Trade on the U. S. Foreign Investment Account

An Atlantic Free Trade Area would not directly affect the degree of freedom of capital movement. But the elimination of government restrictions on merchandise trade is likely to have indirect repercussions on factor movements; primarily on capital, the most mobile factor of all. (It is not expected that the freedom of labor mobility would increase as a result of AFTA.) Our concern will be with the flow of direct—not portfolio—investments.

Table 10

Value of United States Direct Foreign Investments, 1960

	Value ($ billions)	Percentage					
		Mining and Smelting	Petroleum	Manufacturing	Trade	Other	All
Canada	10.2	10.7	24.2	44.8	5.5	14.7	100
Latin America	8.2	15.8	36.8	15.9	7.6	23.9	100
Europe	5.3	0.1	27.4	55.2	11.0	5.4	100
Other Areas	6.0	5.8	60.6	14.8	3.9	15.0	100
All Areas	29.7	10.0	35.0	33.0	7.0	15.0	100

SOURCE: Pizer and Cutler, *U. S. Business Investments in Foreign Countries* (U. .S Department of Commerce, 1962). See also various issues of the *Survey of Current Business,* U. S. Department of Commerce.

In 1960, the value of U. S. direct investments abroad was $30 billion, with the distribution among regions and industries as shown in Table 10. By 1964, the total value of these holdings increased to $44.3 billion, of which $13.8 billion was located in Canada, $0.6 billion in Japan, and $12 billion in Western Europe. Of the latter figure, $5.4 billion was in the EEC and $4.5 billion in the United Kingdom.

Investments of course involve a two-way traffic. And in terms of total holdings (direct and portfolio combined), European investments in the United States in 1964 approximated American investments in Europe. But two-thirds of the European holdings were of the portfolio type and most of the remaining third was concentrated in the service sector (finance, insurance, etc.), rather than in manufacturing. American foreign investments, on the other hand, are largely in the nonservice industries. More important than the stock of holdings at a given point of time is the contrast between the *flow* of investment capital in the two directions. While the value of U. S. investments in Europe nearly tripled during 1957-1964, European investments in the United States increased by only 50 percent. Thus, the major flow of investment capital within AFTA during the past decade has been from the United States to foreign countries. Indeed, on the basis of apriori reasoning, one would expect capital to move from a country with the highest capital-labor ratio to countries in which this ratio is lower. Such a movement would be profitable to the individual investor, and at the same time improve the allocation of resources in the world as a whole. The question facing us is how the establishment of AFTA would influence U. S. foreign investment decisions, and how the anticipated changes in overseas investments would affect the U. S. balance of payments.

Chapter 7

Motives for Direct Investments Abroad

Both economic analysis and empirical studies trace the underlying motive for overseas investments to long-run profit expectations. American enterprises invest in foreign countries when the profit prospects from such investments exceed those anticipated from alternative uses of the funds. From the viewpoint of the national economy, the alternative uses consist of investments in the United States either by the same company or by others who, by obtaining access to those funds, can attain control over real resources. Thus, when investment funds flow to foreign countries, it may be assumed that given the investment climate at home and abroad, expected profits (allowing for the risk factor) from an incremental investment activity in foreign countries exceeds that expected from such activity in the United States. Factors affecting the relative investments climate include: the general level of economic activity, existing and anticipated tax and tariff policies, and general institutional arrangements.

But while such a statement lends itself to analysis with the economists' tool kit, it is too superficial for the understanding of business behavior under diverse circumstances. Indeed, when questioned directly about their motives, business organizations may not even mention increased profits as a reason.[1] Rather, they tend to emphasize

---

[1]See, for example, R. Mikesell, *U. S. Private and Government Investments Abroad* (Eugene, Oregon: University of Oregon Press, 1962), pp. 88-91.

other factors, which in turn have direct or indirect bearing on net earnings. It is important to unravel these basic motivations before one can evaluate the impact of foreign investments.

The factors which contribute to the increased net earnings from foreign investments are so numerous and diverse as to defy an exhaustive survey. At the risk of some oversimplification, I shall lump them into two broad categories. The first category comprises cost or supply considerations, which lower costs of production and distribution, while the second group includes market or demand considerations which influence profits by raising total revenue. While this dichotomy is not clear-cut, and some factors can be classified under either heading, it does correspond to the usual treatment of profit as the difference between revenue and cost.

A. COST CONSIDERATIONS

The desire to increase profits through a reduction in costs certainly plays an important role in foreign investment decisions. It is useful to distinguish between two types of cost-reducing investments. The first arises from the need to obtain raw materials from abroad. Such materials may either be unavailable at home, or obtainable only at extremely high costs. But they are essential to the production and sale of final products at home or abroad. Profit opportunities would remain unexploited without them. Indeed, the vast American foreign investments in the extractive industries are motivated by the fact that the capital must go where the resources are. In a very real sense, the product of such investments is a *complementary* factor of production to the labor and capital employed within the United States. Any diminution in the availability of this resource would directly harm the productivity and remuneration of the latter two factors. This complementary resource includes primary materials, certain agricultural commodities (e.g., tropical products), and some semiprocessed goods brought back to the United States for further processing, with the final product marketed either here or abroad. Inclusion of the last item is dictated by the transportation costs of the primary products. When they are prohibitive or very high, the first stage of processing may have to be done at or near the extraction site, and the product brought home in a semiprocessed form. Investments in foreign transport and communication links, which make possible (or cheapen) exports from the home country to otherwise isolated regions, can also be regarded in the same light. Much of American investment in underdeveloped countries is so motivated.

The second type of cost-reducing investments involves cost other than materials, primarily labor. Although to the company management it makes little difference where costs are cut, the national interest is likely to be differently affected. In the extractive industries case, the resource whose cost is reduced is complementary to U. S. factors of production, raises the productivity of American labor as well as capital, and often leads to increased production within the United States. On the other hand, when foreign investments are designed to lower labor costs, the savings occur in the employment of factors which are competitive with American resources. While such foreign investments raise the productivity of American capital, they tend to lower the productivity of American labor compared to similar investments in the United States.

Perhaps the most potent motive in the second category is a desire to take advantage of lower labor costs in foreign countries. The fact that wage rates in the United States are higher than those abroad is not in itself an indication of higher labor costs. It is simply a reflection of the higher productivity of American labor. But when the wage differentials are not fully offset by productivity differentials, the result is lower labor cost in foreign countries. Industries in which the labor component is high relative to the capital component (namely, the relatively labor intensive industries) would be the first candidates for such cost differentials. But at times an unfavorable labor-cost differential may appear even in capital intensive industries, when wage rates abroad lag considerably behind increases in productivity. The remarkable wage stability in Europe during the second half of the 1950's certainly contributed to that phenomenon, while a reverse trend may have existed in the early 1960's, as the tight labor market in many European countries had a growing impact on wage rates. Another reversal may have been in the making in the mid-1960's as the period of unused industrial capacity in the United States was giving way to labor shortages. Labor cost differentials can be exploited by producing abroad, with the final product sold in the host country, in third countries, and even back in the United States.

Another type of saving that can be secured by manufacturing abroad is transportation costs.. When the final product is perishable, or has a high weight-to-value ratio, proximity to the main markets becomes very important. It may then be advantageous to replace exports by foreign production.

Government policies often play a direct role in inducing foreign investments. The outflow of capital may be motivated by a desire to take advantage of special tax treatment. More often, tariff policies both here and abroad bring about substantial relocations of plants. Successive reductions of duties by the United States can induce companies to produce abroad for sale in the United States. As the American manufacturer loses his protective tariff he may not be able to compete against lower cost imports, primarily of labor intensive products. Consequently he would set up production facilities in low cost areas, from which to supply the American market. For similar reasons, the establishment of the EEC and EFTA in Europe has provided very strong incentive for investing in the two areas. First, such investments enable the producer to circumvent the discriminatory tariff wall he must face when exporting from the United States. And second, since each of the two regional groupings provides a large tariff-free market, a single facility in one foreign location can supply several national markets. Thus, the plant can be large enough to realize economies of scale and the benefits of specialization. Indeed, a survey conducted by the National Industrial Conference Board[2] among U. S. firms that have operations abroad showed that costs in domestic plants are generally lower in cases where the foreign plant's capacity is less than one-tenth of the U. S. plant; costs become nearly equal as the 10 percent level is reached, while costs in foreign operations are lower than in the United States in 85 percent of the cases when the output of plants abroad exceeds one-half of that in the domestic plants.

On the other hand, tariff reduction in foreign countries has the opposite effect of making U. S. exports more competitive abroad, thus lessening the need to produce in foreign countries. In this case, export trade from the United States replaces the potential outward movement of capital.

Once a large company goes abroad, it sometimes becomes necessary for the enterprises which supply it at home to set up overseas branches, in order to provide orderly supplies to the foreign subsidiaries.

---

[2]See T. R. Gates and F. Linden, *Costs and Competition: American Experience Abroad* (New York: The Conference Board, August, 1961).

B. Marketing Considerations[3]

On an abstract level, there exists a historical pattern whereby firms are induced to set up foreign branches as they become familiar with foreign markets through exports. The general widening of business horizons attendant upon the expansion of international trade lead businessmen to increase their foreign investments. But sheer familiarity is merely an enabling condition. The desire to cater to specific market needs appears to be the real motivation. Initially, dissatisfaction with distribution techniques abroad may stimulate the establishment of a selling organization, including warehousing and service facilities, to market exports from the United States. As a second stage the company is inclined to set up production or assembly and conversion plants in order to be close to its customers, provide better services, and gear its product lines to local demands in specific markets. The more complex the product, the greater the advantage of the proximity of the manufacturing plant. At times foreign facilities are set up to satisfy the nationalistic feelings of the customers (or of the local government) and increase their acceptance of the product. However, nationalistic feelings also work in the reverse direction; recent French, Canadian, and even British reactions indicate that real or imaginary disadvantages to the host country have created some aversion to American control of manufacturing facilities.

More generally, the expansion of foreign facilities may be regarded as an integral part of the growth pattern of the firm that tries to maintain its position in the international market and capture at least a constant share of the rapidly increasing foreign market. The United States antitrust legislation provides a powerful inducement in this direction. A firm which has the financial resources to expand through the acquisition of its competitors may be prevented by law from gaining a dominant position in the domestic market. Thus the purchase of foreign firms becomes an important avenue of expansion.

---

[3]For a detailed discussion of these factors see National Industrial Conference Board, *U. S. Production Abroad and the Balance of Payments* (New York, 1966), Chs. 3 and 4. I might add that I do not accept the "organic approach" enunciated by that publication as an explanation of the basic motivation for U. S. foreign investments.

Chapter 8

Trade Liberalization and Capital Movements

The complexity and diversity of the influences outlined in the previous chapter preclude an a priori judgment concerning the effect of AFTA on American foreign investments. The basic theoretical tenet, that factor and commodity movements are partial substitutes for each other,[4] would lead one to expect a reduction in capital outflow from the United States (the relatively capital abundant country) if free trade were established among the major trading nations. But the theory is based on a simplified model, embodying all the traditional Heckscher-Ohlin assumptions, and cannot account for all the counter-forces that may come into play. An empirical answer must therefore be sought.

But because of the hypothetical nature of the problem, it is not possible to resolve it by reliance on past data. Yet it is imperative to shed light on the relative strength of the conflicting influences outlined in the previous chapter. In order to gain such an insight, a questionnaire, reproduced in Appendix III-A, was sent to over 2,000 producing firms listed in the *1964 Directory of American Firms Operating in Foreign Countries*.[5] In it, the respondents were asked to indi-

---

[4]By this we mean that if commodity trade is restricted by governmental or other actions, its place would be taken, in part, by movement of capital and other factors. Conversely, restrictions placed on international factor mobility would tend to stimulate commodity trade. See R. A. Mundell, "International Trade and Factor Mobility," *American Economic Review*, June, 1957, pp. 321-35.

[5]New York, World Trade Academy Press, 1964.

cate how an Atlantic Free Trade Area would affect their foreign investments decisions and the disposition of their foreign earnings. The questions related only to direct investments and did not dwell on the portfolio type.

On the face of it, the universe selected would appear to impart a downward bias to the flow of foreign investments. If only the firms already operating abroad are queried, possible new entrants into foreign production activities are excluded out of hand. It turned out, however, that the *Directory* includes many firms which are merely doing foreign business rather than being engaged in direct overseas production. At most, only one-fifth of them had direct control over manufacturing facilities. In all probability, the universe included most American firms with a horizon wide enough to contemplate foreign investments.

Altogether, 191 replies were received, of which 22 did not answer the questions for various reasons. The 169 usable questionnaires represent close to one-half of the large companies with direct production interests abroad.[6] Although they cannot be regarded as a representative sample in a statistical sense, they do offer a qualitative view of the factors affecting foreign investment decisions under the projected AFTA.

It is possible to divide the 169 valid replies as follows: 82 firms stated that an AFTA would have no effect on their foreign investments decisions; 46 responding companies expected either to contract their foreign manufacturing operations or avoid an otherwise contemplated expansion in the event of an AFTA; and finally, 41 firms anticipated an expansion of their foreign production facilities to follow from the establishment of an AFTA. These categories cannot be distinguished on the basis of products or product lines, since many industries are represented in all three.

Equally significant to the quantitative breakdown, are the reasons, arguments, and general discussion contained in the replies, which yield important insights into business thinking. Since many of the respondents did not advance any reasoning for their answer, the qualitative analysis is based on fewer than the total number of replies.

---

[6]The National Industrial Conference Board Study, *Cost and Competition: American Experience Abroad,* is based on the experience of 147 firms with foreign production facilities.

A. Firms Expecting No Change

For the most part, companies which expected the AFTA to have no effect on their operations abroad stated that tariffs and related obstacles were insignificant elements in their competitive posture. Some are resource-oriented industries, and must produce where the raw materials are; others produce perishable products; but many emphasized transport cost as the overwhelming impediment to trade, dwarfing tariffs in importance. Following are a couple of illustrations of such responses.

A manufacturer of heating, plumbing, and air conditioning products stated:

Generally speaking, our products are heavy and the freight element is more important than duties, tariffs. . . . We believe that a possible "Atlantic Free Trade Area" would have little effect on our operations.

A chemical producer wrote:

Since transportation costs are large in relation to the selling prices of our products and since raw materials are in general available within each country involved in your study or are close at hand, local manufacture is imperative to meet local competition.

Similar responses were given by a score of other firms, producing a variety of products. But the majority of the respondents in this category did not specify a reason at all. Most of these companies also indicated that an AFTA would not affect the disposition of their foreign earnings.

Several firms under this classification, emphasized that the "no effect" reply applied only to their overall foreign investments position. They do expect significant changes in the production composition of their facilities as well as in their overseas locations, both aimed at the attainment of lower costs. Two of them anticipate consolidation of a few plants into one large and more efficient facility, from which several markets can be supplied. It appears that Canada would be a principal loser from such a transformation. Several examples of these responses are presented below:

We would contract in the ECM and expand in Japan on the basis of free market into ECM from Japan and lower manufacturing costs in Japan. This would not affect the total of our foreign investment but would reallocate it. *(printing machinery)*

Rather than expand existing manufacturing facilities in Canada, which necessarily supply a restricted market, consideration would be given to the most advantageous area in which to produce any additional volume or even relocate present operations. *(chemicals)*

Our product line—largely variable resistors, switches, and micro-electronic components and circuits—is easily transported and contains a relatively small percentage of material costs in relation to capital and labor costs. Without an Atlantic FTA we would tend to build general purpose plants in countries having large, growing markets. With an Atlantic FTA we would probably build specialized plants in countries with cheap production costs. For example, those products using high capital and low labor inputs would be made in specialized plants in a low cost capital area such as the U. S. But products requiring a large labor input would be made in specialized plants in low cost labor areas such as Ireland or Hong Kong. *Thus an Atlantic FTA would cause us to be more resource oriented and less market oriented* in selecting investment sites. *(electronic components)*

Our company has food manufacturing plants in the United States, Canada, United Kingdom, France, Switzerland and Germany. While we are in the same general industry in all of these countries, we do not manufacture identical product lines in each of these countries. An Atlantic Free Trade Area would permit us to introduce our French line of goods for instance into the United States at a price basis which would be economic and competitive. The ultimate consequence of this introduction must be the establishment in the United States of manufacturing facilities capable of producing a part of the French items here. Similarly we would be able to introduce on a mass price basis certain of our United States items into Europe and in due course they would be supported on the continent with manufacturing facilities there. *(food products)*

If we had free trade with Canada our Western U. S. plant could serve Western Canada—freight savings would offset increased labor costs, but the Canadian plant would cut into U. S. eastern market. *(piping systems)*

As you point out duties are only one factor in such decisions. The others, including specifically the ability to pick up a telephone and place an order for immediate delivery or obtain prompt service after the sale, are of equal influence in buyer motivation. Consequently, except as distinguished by market proximity, again the case of Canada, this company's planned foreign investments would not be substantially affected. Limited item manufacturers of standard products, such as adding machines etc. could limit their foreign operations to warehousing sales and service. This would not be true for speciality chemical producers with hundreds of products in the line all having limited shelf life. *(chemicals)*

B. Firms Expecting Contraction

Of the 46 firms which expect contraction in the event of an AFTA, some indicated that they would actually reduce their foreign operations. But many stated that while existing facilities would remain intact "because cost to get out is too great," the contemplated expansion programs would be avoided. Several firms wrote that in the event of AFTA they would consolidate their foreign manufacturing operations. Europe, for example, could then be served from one or two locations, thus eliminating the need, now made necessary by the tariff, for plants in many individual countries. Respondents often stressed that an AFTA would lead to economies of scale and more efficient production, as facilities are consolidated in a way dictated by cost consideration. More rational production patterns would then follow.

The reason given for these changes was invariably clear-cut and directly traceable to the tariff. The elimination of tariffs under an AFTA would increase the competitiveness of American exports making it unnecessary to produce abroad. Thus commodity trade would partly replace capital movements. A few direct quotations to that effect will serve to illustrate the point:

We could supply our Canadian market at less expense from our U. S. factories if tariffs were eliminated. We would prefer to serve our customers in the EFTA area and the other countries of Western Europe outside of EEC from our plant in Holland. *(hydraulic cylinders)*

Re Japan—now contemplating establishment of Japanese mfg. facilities because duty and freight preclude extensive sales ex USA. Would establish only a sales office in Japan if 30 percent duty were eliminated. *(valves)*

If we had not established manufacturing facilities in Holland recently (1960) an Atlantic FTA might well cause us to avoid such an undertaking. *(sewing machines)*

The high duties on our machines in England forces us to manufacture there. *(cutting machines)*

In a long product line business many of the low volume items would be manufactured in USA for economy reasons—hence diminishing the development of facilities in Canada. *(pens)*

With tariff eliminated it would almost surely be more economical to supply our Canadian requirements for electrical appliances from U. S. plants. We will shortly consider the establishment of common market plants for both appliances and machinery. Tariff is a major cost factor and might make it practical to supply the common market from existing U. S. and Scottish plants. Elimination of common market tariff on appliances and machinery would improve our competitive position on both products from present plants and would encourage greater sales effort. *(textile machinery)*

By being able economically to concentrate manufacturing of trackless equipment in the United States, removing that product line from France and Great Britain, it would eliminate the major production in France and leave manufacturing facilities free in Britain to absorb the remainder of manufacturing done in France. With elimination of tariffs going into Common Market countries, the desirability of manufacturing capability in France would disappear. The trend in the Common Market countries appears to be towards higher prices, wages, and costs generally as against an apparently better control of economic factors in Britain. *(industrial machinery)*

We could probably service our Canadian needs, or at least a large portion of those needs, from our manufacturing facilities in the United States. *(records)*

Elimination of duties and import restrictions would eliminate the need for local manufacture thus permitting higher volume and resultant cost reductions in other plants which could supply the area. *(household appliances)*

Any foreign manufacturing undertaking contemplates lower selling price, and duty elimination would make lower costs questionable. *(chemical products)*

Ours is a technical product wherein our knowhow is valuable. If no duties— could compete successfully by export—from here. However, our already made investment would stay—as cost to get out too great—and could maintain our position in market by advantage of no freight and national pride— in the foreign country we are located in now. *(elastic fabrics)*

Commodity production of higher value/weight ratio would be concentrated here. Specialities, with high service or adjustment to use, more probably would be expanded abroad. *(chemicals)*

The combination of ocean freight plus Japanese, common market, and EFTA duties and related taxes may require us to commence assembly and later manufacture some products within these markets. If duties and related taxes were eliminated it is doubtful whether freight savings alone would be sufficient inducement. In general because of volume plus automation we find our U. S. costs very competitive. In addition when rapidly rising labor costs abroad are considered this is further reason to be reluctant to manufacture abroad. *(product unspecified)*

Present U. S. facilities adequate to fill market demands but tariff barriers in certain common market countries require that our product be manufactured in those countries if we are to remain price competitive. *(linotype machines)*

On the assumption that an Atlantic FTA is created which would eliminate all trade restrictions, we would probably undertake to serve some markets through existing manufacturing facilities rather than the creation of new units. This would be particularly true in Canada for certain parts of the market could be served advantageously through our domestic factories and in Europe where some of the FTA countries could purchase from our existing locations. *(industrial and automotive belts)*

With the elimination of all trade restrictions (including tariffs, quotas, etc.) on manufactured commodities in an area encompassing the U. S., Canada, Western Europe, and Japan, it is entirely possible that because of the facilities we have in the U. S. and the large volume of products which normally can be manufactured here at costs lower than abroad, we would export those products having a high dollar value per cubic foot and discontinue their manufacture overseas. It is also possible that because of the cost of ocean freight we would continue in the areas named to manufacture products having a low dollar value per cubic foot and possibly those products having a very high labor content in their cost. In other words, there might be some contraction in the dollar volume of overseas manufacture and a shift in the type of products made abroad. In the interest of manufacturing at the lowest possible cost in these areas, it is entirely possible that the remainder of the product that would be left for local manufacture would be consolidated into one location, thereby eliminating or changing the present outlook. *(air conditioning and refrigeration systems)*

These responses apply to most foreign areas of manufacture. The EEC is often mentioned, probably because of the tariff discrimination. But the most frequently mentioned area of contemplated contraction is Canada, a market which can be readily serviced from stateside locations. In addition to easy accessability and low transport costs, costs of production there are similar to those prevailing in the United States. Thus a producer of electronic components stated:

Time, distance, shipping costs, etc., are no real problem in dealing with Canadian business. If duties were eliminated, we would deal with Canada on the same basis as a "51st state." This would not be true in the EEC, EFTA or Japan where we feel we would still have to maintain manufacturing facilities—although they might well be planned to be less independent of U. S. components, etc., than is the case at present.

Most respondents in this category also indicated that they would increase repatriation of foreign earnings, because less would be needed for expansion purposes: "More remittance back here simply because if none or slower expansion of manufacturing abroad—less need to reinvest profits." *(elastic fabrics)* Finally, a great majority of the firms expecting contraction plan to expand their marketing and warehousing facilities abroad, in order to support intensified sales efforts from the United States.

C. Firms Expecting Expansion

Unlike the cases of contraction, many of the 41 firms which expect to expand their foreign production facilities in the event of an AFTA gave ambiguous reasons, or did not relate the anticipated expansion to the AFTA. The relevant reasons can be classified into two groups: Cost considerations and market considerations.

The expansion of trade following the establishment of an AFTA, and the intensification of competition in international markets, would force firms to locate in least cost areas. Since products manufactured in the United States would not always be competitve, some of the production would have to move abroad. In three cases involving relatively labor-intensive products, the foreign expansion was deemed necessary in order to sell in the American market. As American manufacturers lose the protective tariffs, they would not be able to compete against lower cost imports. Consequently they would set up or expand production facilities in low cost areas, from which they would supply the United States. These reasons are documented in the following quotations:

Due to lower labor costs, the cost of manufacturing in our plants in Great Britain is less than in U.S.A., and we therefore would be more competitive or obtain a greater profit. *(electric instruments)*

Unless there was a significant change towards equalizing labor rates, labor productivity and governmental "subsidies" on export trade, much of our United States production would not be competitive with other countries. *(clothing)*

Lower European production costs will require increased facilities abroad, both as a defensive measure, with respect to domestic market, and to permit expansion of foreign sales. *(typesetting machines)*

With completely free trade between the United States and the markets indicated, it will be very difficult in our industry to compete with countries which are currently exporting to the United States due to the dramatically lower wages and salaries presently existing in these countries. *(electronic components)*

With the elimination of even the present rather inadequate protection which the U. S. special steel industry now has against the taking over of the U. S. market by lower cost foreign producers, there would be even greater inroads made by foreign producers in taking over a large share of this U. S. market. Accordingly, there would be reduced incentive for additional investment in manufacturing plants in the United States until such time as wage levels in foreign countries, such as Japan and the Common Market, more nearly approach those in the United States. This would seem to be a long time off. At the same time, there would be encouragement to expand our present foreign joint ventures to at least participate in enterprises whose expansion in the specialty steel field would thereby be greatly encouraged. There would, at the same time, seem to be little incentive to proceed with any investment in Canada, since the market could be probably more efficiently served from the United States or foreign countries. *(steel products)*

The second reason can be articulated as follows: An AFTA would lead to the expansion of trade. Once a company increases its exports, it is drawn to set up production or assembly and conversion facilities abroad so as to be close to its customers, to provide better services, to gear its product lines to local demand, and at times to satisfy the nationalistic feelings of its customers (or of the local government). The following citations illustrate this argument:

Such an AFTA would give us considerable opportunity to further expand distribution in the areas concerned, by initially establishing warehousing and sales organizations. As these develop, consideration could be given to further plant expansion, either of our present plants, or in the areas wherein warehousing proved to be successful. *(floor covering accessories and supplies)*

We find it advisable to have our production facilities close to our customers. Geographically our present plants are well located to handle major markets. Increased opportunity for more trade in given areas would require more capacity at existing locations. *(abrasives)*

Our products, metal office furniture, in most cases are not of sufficient value to justify overseas shipment (given their bulk and unit price). Thus, overseas manufacturing subsidiaries are necessary in order to enter markets outside this hemisphere. Given a FTA, we assume that very shortly European plants and U. S. plants would be invading each other's markets. Thus, we would consider going abroad. *(metal office furniture)*

Decisions on location are primarily based on geographical proximity to our customers. *(containers and packages)*

Although free trade between nations looks good on paper, we feel that the nationalistic approach is still the best. The French will buy from the French, Japan from Japan, Germany from Germans, etc. *(engine bearings)*

Of the various geographical areas, the EEC is mentioned most frequently as the site of possible expansion, followed closely by the EFTA countries. This reflects their potential as important markets, but is also a result of the lower production costs prevailing there. Although Canada and Japan are also mentioned frequently as possible locations for expansion, several firms indicated that they would contract or liquidate their Canadian operation, along with expansion elsewhere, because the Canadian market could (in the event of an AFTA) be supplied better from the United States:

For example, some of our products are produced less expensively in Europe than at our United States plants, so we would probably import these items if there were no restrictions. For other products, exactly the reverse is true. In one case, we might have to increase our investment in France, where in another, we might decrease our investment in Canada. *(equipments)*

There would be little reason for two plants so close together—one in North Central United States and the other in Southern Canada. Therefore, the Canadian manufacturing facilities would probably be liquidated. *(industrial equipments and electronic components)*

If there were no tariff between Canada and the United States, a number of our manufacturing operations in that country would not have been built. *(chemicals)*

Only one company indicated the reverse:

We could supply part of the U. S. market from the Canadian plant. This is impractical now because of the U. S. duties on the products imported from Canada. At present there is no (or little) duty on these products sent to Canada from our U. S. plant. *(pharmaceuticals)*

Although the firms in the "expansion" category expect to use some new U. S. capital, the main sources of funds for the new plants would be reinvested foreign earnings, followed closely by foreign borrowing. Consequently, many responding companies expect a slowdown in the repatriation of earnings to the United States:

Availability of new foreign investment opportunities would probably result in reinvestments in these new areas, rather than repatriation to the U. S. *(fibre containers)*

With less fear of currency fluctuations, we would probably tend to leave more money abroad—assuming a reasonable flowback for dividends after initial expansion costs. *(office furniture)*

With increased opportunity for further expansion, it is possible that a larger proportion of foreign earnings would be reinvested abroad. *(gloves)*

We would expect that there would be a rapid increase in the manufacture of our products in the countries indicated with a corresponding lessening of our manufacturing activities in the United States. It would require re-investment of our earnings abroad to support this expansion of our foreign activities. *(electrical and electronic components)*

D. SUMMARY

It would appear that the forces leading to expansion and contraction are both powerful, making it difficult to determine the net effect. On balance, however, judging from the strength and lucidity of the reasoning offered by the respondents as well as from their numbers, an AFTA may result in a small net contraction of total foreign investments—primarily in Canada (because of its accessibility to stateside facilities) and somewhat in the EEC (probably because of the elimination of tariff discrimination). The forces halting the expansion would be reinforced by nationalistic feelings in France[7] and other

---

[7]See for example, the story in the *N. Y. Times* (July 26, 1964, Financial Section) about the French reaction to the acquisition of France's Machine Bull Company by General Electric; and the account (July 30, 1964) of the British reaction to the Chrysler-Rootes deal.

countries against American control over domestic manufacturing facilities. But more important than the overall effect would be the rationalization of production, involving consolidation of facilities and of product lines, changes in the composition of investments, and shifts in location. Here the main loser of American capital would be Canada. Firms in all three categories, including those contemplating expansion, indicated that they are likely to contract their Canadian operations or avoid expansion in that country.

Chapter 9
Effect on the U. S.
Balance of Payments

Before examining the implications of the anticipated effects of AFTA, it will be useful to survey the general relationship between foreign investments and the external accounts of the United States.

On the face of it, the balance of payments is adversely affected by the amount of the capital outflow. But this oversimplified statement overlooks the relationship between the various balance of payments items, and ignores the fact that capital outflow generates "favorable" movements of both goods and funds. Not much is known about the extent of these interrelationships, and a need for further empirical studies is definitely indicated in this area. However, a penetrating analysis by A. Gerlof Homan,[8] based on Department of Commerce data, provides some insights into the problem.

First, when an American enterprise is established abroad, it immediately generates exports in the form of capital equipments and materials required for the plant's operations. On the average, such sales from the United States constitute about one quarter of the initial investment. Thus, even in the first year of operation a million dollar investment outlay requires a payment outflow of only three-fourths that amount. In subsequent years, the export of spare parts,

---

[8]A. Gerlof Homan, "Some Measures and Interpretations of the Effects of the Operations of U. S. Foreign Enterprises on the U. S. Balance of Payments," a paper presented at the annual meeting of the Western Economic Association at UCLA, August, 1962 (mimeographed).

materials, and additional equipment tends to continue, further mitigating the initial impact on the balance of payments.

Next, there is the return inflow of earnings into the United States. In any given year, this inflow represents earnings on investments made in past years. Put differently, an investment made at a point of time will generate earnings in subsequent years. It has been estimated that on the average, the pay-back period on the original capital outflow (i.e., about three-fourths of the original investment made) is about five years. The estimates range from two years in petroleum up to ten or eleven years in the case of manufacturing and mining and smelting enterprises. Geographically, the pay-back period for Europe is around ten years and more than fifteen years in Canada.

All the three direct effects vary greatly between regions and industries. Quantifying them is a difficult if not an impossible task, but the preliminary attempt of Homan deserves our consideration. Assuming an original investment of $1 million, he concludes that a representative enterprise operating abroad for fifteen years would have the direct effect shown in Table 11. Despite the preliminary (and rough)

Table 11

Net Effect of Foreign Investments on the U. S. Balance of Payments

	All Industries	($ millions) Mining and Smelting	Petroleum	Manu- facturing	Trade
All Areas	—0.2	—10.9	+ 1.8	+1.4	10.9
Canada	—2.9	—23.1	—22.1	—0.1	na
Europe	+3.4	0.0	+ 8.2	+1.0	na
Latin America	—1.2	— 5.3	— 2.3	+3.8	na

SOURCE: A. G. Homan, *op. cit.,* p. 27.

nature of these estimates, they do suggest that within the regions included in AFTA, investments in Europe are most favorable and in Canada least favorable to the U. S. balance of payments.

Finally, we come to the least tangible aspect of foreign investments, namely the sales of the products of American subsidiaries. In 1957 such sales amounted to $38 billion, of which 73 percent was marketed in the host country, 10 percent shipped to the United States, and 17 percent exported to third country destinations (Table 12). There are great variations in these proportions between different industries and countries. But since we do not know what the situation

Table 12

Sales of United States Foreign Enterprises in 1957

	All Industries	Mining	Petroleum	Manufacturing	Agriculture
Total Sales	$38.1 billion	$2.0 billion	$14.5 billion	$18.3 billion	$0.9 billion
In host country	72.6%	16%	66%	84%	37%
Exported to U. S.	9.9%	44%	10%	6%	38%
Exported to third country	17.5%	40%	24%	10%	25%
Canada	$11.7 billion	$0.7 billion	$2.1 billion	$7.9 billion	$0.2 billion
In host country	82%	17%	94%	84%	97%
Exported to U. S.	12%	45%	6%	11%	3%
Exported to third country	6%	29%	0%	5%	0%
Latin America	$7.5 billion	$0.8 billion	$3.0 billion	$2.4 billion	$0.6 billion
In host country	60%	13%	41%	96%	20%
Exported to U. S.	20%	42%	31%	1%	45%
Exported to third country	20%	45%	28%	3%	35%
Europe	$11.2 billion	$0 billion	$4.4 billion	$6.3 billion	$0 billion
In host country	84%		92%	78%	
Exported to U. S.	2%		0%	3%	
Exported to third country	14%		8%	19%	

SOURCE: A. G. Homan, *op. cit.*

would have been in the absence of foreign investments, it is rather difficult to evaluate their efforts.

A large portion of the sales of American subsidiaries to the United States consists of raw materials, agricultural products, and semi-processed goods, which cannot be produced at home, or can be produced only at much higher cost than abroad. Since the United States is dependent on these materials in whole or in part, their importation from American foreign subsidiaries benefits the balance of payments because it lowers the cost of these imports. When it comes to manufacturing imports, the answer depends on whether such sales displace domestically produced products, or products which would have been imported anyway. In the first case the effect on the balance of payments is unfavorable, and in the second case—favorable.

Sales of U. S. subsidiaries in foreign markets (i.e., the host country as well as third countries) present a similar problem with respect to American exports. Sales of foreign mining and agricultural enterprises probably do not affect U. S. exports very much because the United States is a net importer of these products. As regards manufactured products, to the extent that they displace exports from the United States, they have an adverse effect on the balance of payments. But to the extent that they displace actual or potential foreign sources of supply, their impact on the U. S. balance of payments is favorable.[9]

One last point should now be mentioned. Most successful foreign ventures are expanded in subsequent years through the investments of retained earnings and locally borrowed funds. Correspondingly, their book value rises substantially.[10] These assets are obviously not available to the American monetary authorities in coping with the balance of payments deficit (which is essentially a liquidity problem). But they do strengthen the long-run creditor position of the United States. As such, they inspire at least some additional confidence in the dollar as an international reserve currency. Correspondingly, they have some intangible (and unmeasurable) value in contributing to our ability to run current deficits with relative impunity. Thus although the accumulated assets of American foreign subsidiaries do not help directly with the immediate deficit problem, they should not be ignored in assessing the impact of foreign investments on the balance of payments.

We are now in position to inquire specifically about the impact of AFTA on the external capital account of the United States. It was concluded in the previous chapter that AFTA would cause a shift in the location of American foreign investments from Canada to Europe. Taking only the three direct effects, it now appears that an average of all U. S. enterprises in Europe generated substantial net receipts over a fifteen-year period, while in Canada the average produced net U. S. payments. This conclusion applies to each of the three broad sectors for which data are available. In other words, the overall difference observed here is not a result (or at least not wholly a result)

---

[9]A recent survey by the National Industrial Conference Board found that "often production was begun abroad in order to avoid losing exports that were threatened with local competition or local import barriers of some kind." Reported in the *Wall Street Journal*, March 28, 1966.

[10]Book value of U. S. foreign affiliates increased from $12 billions in 1950 to $50 billions in 1965.

of the different composition of U. S. investments in the two regions. Therefore the anticipated changes resulting from AFTA would be favorable to the U. S. balance of payments.

The effects of the sales of foreign subsidiaries are more difficult to determine. It would appear from the survey discussed in Chapter 8 that the main reason for the shift from Canada to other locations would be the ability to supply the Canadian market from stateside facilities in the absence of the tariff. That would contribute further to the improvement of the U. S. external position. On the other hand, the expanded sales from other locations would worsen the balance of payments, making the net indirect effect indeterminate. However, if we assume that the reduced[11] sales from Canadian locations would be fully compensated for by sales from the United States, while the increased sales from other locations (e.g., Europe) would not fully displace American exports, the presumption is that the indirect effects would also be favorable to the United States. It should be noted, however, that the favorable effect may be counteracted to some extent by Canadian feedback. Inasmuch as the Canadian imports from the United States depend on the availability of American dollars, the direct effect may induce Canada to reduce its purchases of American products. On balance, if we weigh the long run, these considerations point to an improvement in the U. S. external position resulting from the anticipated shifts in foreign investments locations.

---

[11]The word "reduced" (increased) in this context does not necessarily mean a reduction in absolute amount. Rather, it may mean "lower" (higher) by comparison with what the magnitude would have been in the absence of an AFTA.

Appendix III

FOREIGN INVESTMENT QUESTIONNAIRE
POSSIBLE EFFECTS OF AN ATLANTIC FREE TRADE AREA
ON U. S. CAPITAL FLOWS

PURPOSE:

The Council on Foreign Relations is engaged in a broad study of alternative arrangements for trade liberalization in the Atlantic Community. As part of this study, the present survey is designed to assemble information on the possible effects of an Atlantic Free Trade Area (AFTA) on the long-run capital account of the U. S. balance of payments. The questionnaire is directed to American companies which engage in production activities both here and abroad. It relies exclusively on informed management opinion concerning the operations of their own companies.

CONFIDENTIAL HANDLING:

The information you supply will be treated in *strict confidence*. It will not be used in any way permitting identification of your firm. Your cooperation in answering the questions will be appreciated.

SCOPE:

A variety of factors influence corporate decisions to engage in manufacturing activities abroad. Cost considerations, foreign laws and governmental policies, consumer attitudes and tastes, tariffs and other forms of trade restrictions, the existence of regional groupings, all play a role in the decision to establish or expand foreign plants.

In this survey you are asked to concentrate *only on one factor* influencing the investment decision, assuming no change in all others:

106

The elimination of all trade restrictions (including tariffs, quotas, etc.) on manufactured commodities in an area encompassing the United States, Canada, Western Europe and Japan. We would like to know what effect the creation of such a Free Trade Area would have on your *decisions concerning the location of your production facilities and the disposition of foreign earnings.*

Investment Decisions

(I) *No change*

☐ An Atlantic FTA is unlikely to affect our foreign investment decisions.

(II) *Contraction*

An Atlantic FTA is likely to induce us to:

☐ (1) Contract our manufacturing facilities abroad.

☐ (2) Avoid an otherwise contemplated expansion of our manufacturing facilities abroad.

Location

The contraction (or avoidance of contemplated expansion) will take place in:

☐ (1) Canada

☐ (2) The European Common Market countries

☐ (3) The countries of the European Free Trade Area Association

☐ (4) Other European countries

☐ (5) Japan

☐ (6) Other_____
Specific geographical area

Reasons:
Please state the reasons underlying that decision.

(III) *Expansion*

An Atlantic FTA is likely to induce us to (check one or more):

☐ (1) Establish new manufacturing facilities abroad.

☐ (2) Expand existing manufacturing facilities abroad.

☐ (3) Establish sales subsidiaries with new warehousing facilities, but with the products supplied from our home plants.

Location

The expansion will take place in:

☐ (1) Canada

☐ (2) The European Common Market countries.

☐ (3) The countries of the European Free Trade Area Association.

☐ (4) Other European countries

☐ (5) Japan

☐ (6) Other_____
Specific geographical area

Reasons:
Please state the reasons underlying that decision.

(IV) *Shifts in Manufacturing Facilities:*

Would the foregoing entail a shift of your manufacturing facilities from one foreign country to another?

☐ Yes   ☐ No

If *yes,* please specify the nature of the shift and indicate reasons:

(V) *Sources of Funds:*

The source of funds for the proposed expansion will be:

☐ New U. S. capital.

☐   Reinvested earnings.

☐   Borrowing abroad.

       Other_____
                    Specific geographical area

(VI) *Disposition of Foreign Earnings:*
Would an Atlantic FTA affect the disposition of your foreign earnings as between:

      Repatriation to the U. S.

      Reinvestments abroad

      Retaining the funds abroad in liquid form
         ☐ Yes   ☐ **No**

Please state the nature of the change and the reasons for it:

Products produced by your company in foreign countries:

Foreign countries in which you operate production facilities:

APPENDIX III-B

DIRECT FOREIGN INVESTMENTS AND U. S. REAL INCOME

Since the main thrust of the U. S. government balance of payments policy has been in the area of direct foreign investments, it is of interest to dwell on the various effects of such investments. The analysis in Chapter 9 suggests that over the long run direct foreign investments are likely to affect the balance of payments favorably. Thus the impact of any program restricting the outflow of investment capital may be self defeating. Of course the concern of U. S. policy is with the immediate future. But at the time of writing (early 1967) we are already witnessing the third annual extension (and toughening) of the "voluntary" restraints on foreign investments by the Commerce Department. And the longer the program lasts—the more likely it is to backfire. After all, the long run is made up of several successive short runs. Whatever the temporary benefits to the balance of payments, they are achieved at a substantial cost to our future payments position.

But restrictions of foreign investments can be justified on another ground, viz., the maximization of U. S. real income. Free factor mobility (primarily capital) is the optimal policy from the viewpoint of maximizing world-wide real product. But it has different effects on the capital exporting and the host countries. The latter nations certainly derive immense benefits from the infusion of foreign capital. Among those benefits are the increase in capital/labor ratio which raises labor productivity, the contribution to government's revenue through corporate taxes, the intensification of competition in the product and factor markets, and the general modernization of the economy. Foreign capital usually brings with it technical and managerial know-how, thereby improving the organization of production and distribution. It introduces new products which not only enhance consumer satisfaction, but—because they include new industrial instruments—also increase the efficacy of production. Even those who complain about excessive control of certain branches of their economy by American capital,[12] or about the interferences of American subsidiaries with the realization of a national economic plan, do not deny the

---

[12]A recent report in the *New York Times* (dated March 16, 1966) however, suggests that this adverse reaction may not be as widespread as commonly believed. It is based on a survey by the Atlantic Council in 8 European countries, which found a "favorable climate" for U. S. business investments in most cases.

immense contribution made by U. S. capital to the national economies of the host nations.

But what is the effect of direct foreign investments on the real income of the capital exporting country, namely the United States?[13] In order to isolate this from other related problems, we shall assume that the economy is operating at full employment, and is continuously maintained at or about that level by fiscal and monetary means. Also, the balance of payments is assumed to be in equilibrium, and to adjust rapidly and smoothly to transfers of capital. The question posed under these circumstances is how to distribute the aggregate savings generated by a fully employed economy between domestic and foreign investments[14] so as to maximize real national product (or income). Put differently, will real national product be maximized if the distribution is left strictly to market decisions exercised by a multitude of profit maximizing enterprises—namely, if the location of each investment project would depend on expected after-tax earnings here and abroad? The answer is that particularly in the manufacturing sector, foreign investments are likely to proceed considerably beyond what is warranted by the *national* interest; and this for several reasons.

First, there are several types of risks which the firm may not fully account for before going abroad: The risk of unfavorable public regulations, such as regulations of profits, repudiation of loans, or even confiscation, affect the individual firm equally if its investments are at home or abroad. But the national economy suffers only if the investments are abroad.

Second, there is a revenue loss to the government of the United States. In order to avoid double taxation (i.e., on grounds of equity), foreign investors are usually permitted to credit income taxes paid abroad against their domestic tax liability. In deciding where to invest,

---

[13]The recent literature on this topic includes: (a) Paul B. Simpson, "Foreign Investments and the National Economic Advantage: A Theoretical Analysis," *U. S. Private and Government Investments Abroad,* ed. R. F. Micksell (Eugene: University of Oregon Press, 1962), pp. 503-27. (b) J. Cater Murphy, "International Investments and the National Interest," *The Southern Economic Journal,* July, 1960. (c) A. E. Jasay, "The Social Choice Between Home and Overseas Investments," *The Economic Journal,* March 1960. (d) Marvin Frankel "Home versus Foreign Investments: A Case Against Capital Export," *Kyklos,* 1965, pp. 411-33.

[14]The full employment assumption is important at this point. If the economy suffers from considerable unemployment because of insufficient demand, then foreign investments have little or no opportunity cost in terms of foregone domestic investments. All that is important in this case is to channel domestic savings into investments, be they foreign or domestic.

the private firm compares expected after-tax profit here and abroad, since it is a matter of indifference to it which government receives the tax. But with corporate taxes ranging up to 48 percent of earnings, and constituting a major portion of government revenue, this is a major concern to the national government. Under present institutional arrangements, foreign investments benefit the national interest only if *after-tax* profits abroad exceed net earnings *before* taxes in the United States. To some extent this fiscal loss is offset by the need for public expenditures to service home investments; a need which is absent in the case of foreign investments.

Third, investments affect the productivity and remunerations of capital as well as of labor and land.[15] An addition to the capital stock, whether here or abroad, has the following effects: (a) total real output will rise as an increasing volume of capital is combined with a relatively stable amount of other resources, mainly labor and land; (b) the productivity of the incremental unit of capital, and therefore the rate of return to existing capital, will tend to decline as the capital stock rises in proportion to other factors; and (c) the productivity of labor and land, and their rate of remuneration, would tend to increase as each unit of these resources is combined with an increasing volume of capital in the productive process. The private firm is concerned only with the rate of return on capital when deciding where to locate its investment. The national view, on the other hand, cannot overlook the implications to other factors of production. In the case of foreign investments, it is the productivity of foreign labor and land that would rise. If the investments are undertaken at home, these benefits accrue to domestic resources.

Furthermore, the expansion of production attendant upon the new investments usually carries with it indirect benefits. These include improvement in the quality of labor, better production methods and techniques, and superior forms of organization. In the case of foreign investments, these benefits would be lost to the domestic economy. Indeed, since foreign investments usually require American technical and managerial talent, the movement of such personnel abroad deprives the U. S. economy of their services.

---

[15]In this connection it is important to note that American foreign investments in the mid-1960's constitute an increment to the vast amounts of capital already held by American companies abroad (amounting to tens of billions of dollars). Thus any addition to this capital stock tends to lower the rate of return on the already existing capital.

This loss to the domestic economy may be more than offset in many instances by one important factor: the productivity of domestic capital and other resources depends in some measure on the capital endowment of the rest of the world. This phenomenon is most evident in the case of foreign investments in the extractive industries. The provision of primary materials for foreign sources (when domestic sources are not available) increases the productivity of domestic factors of production, since such materials are complementary to American capital and labor. In this case, there is a gain rather than a loss to domestic factors. Since a large share of U. S. investment in underdeveloped countries tends to concentrate in the extractive industries, the foreign policy objective of promoting investments in these areas (either as a substitute or in addition to foreign aid) happens to coincide with the domestic economic interest.

On the other hand, over half of our investments in developed countries (primarily western Europe) is concentrated in manufacturing industries. Here the argument outlined in the previous paragraph holds only to a limited extent. It is therefore suggested that foreign investments, motivated by private profits considerations, would exceed the amount justified by the national interest. In all probability, profit after taxes earned abroad should exceed profits before taxes earned at home in order for the national interest to be satisfied. Left to business judgments alone, the amount of American investments in foreign manufacturing industries would exceed that justified on national economic grounds.

This is a fairly short-run analysis. In the long run, American investments would increase income and output in the receiving countries, inducing increased imports from the United States. American output and employment would thereby be favorably affected. These benefits have not been included in the above considerations.

Finally, the above argument constitutes strictly a one-sided view of America's stake in international investments. The other side of the coin is investments by foreigners in American manufacturing industries. In this case, all the indirect benefits accrue to the United States, while the investments process proceeds beyond what is warranted from the foreign national point of view. However, we have seen that the main flow of direct investment capital is from the United States to foreign countries.

Can the voluntary restraints program be justified on the grounds of national economic interest—namely, the desire to restrict the outflow of investment capital to a level below that induced by private profit considerations? If so, this would call for permanent rather than temporary restrictions. As in the case of tariffs, such action might invite retaliation from other countries, in the process of which all might lose, and the international financial system would be severely impaired.

Considering our international responsibilites, U. S. policy should not be based on the narrow consideration of maximizing domestic real income. In my view there should be no restrictions on foreign investments—voluntary or compulsory. But if a restrictive program is undertaken, for whatever reason, the most efficient approach should be adopted. The current voluntary restraints constitute an inefficient method for accomplishing the desired objective. The program essentially imposes a quota on the annual level of capital outflow of each of one thousand participating companies. What determines whether or not a desired investment will be made is not only the anticipated flow of net earnings. Rather, it is the amount of foreign investments undertaken by the company during some predetermined base period. Thus it is perfectly possible for the most profitable investment outlets to go begging, while less profitable opportunities are being exploited. Such a procedure is injurious both to the national economic interest and to the balance of payments position.

If restrictions are to be imposed, then both points of view dictate a totally different approach. The scheme must insure that foreign investments will be undertaken only if the anticipated returns exceed domestic earnings by a certain optimal amount. That can best be achieved by the imposition of an optimal capital export tax. Since we do not know the level of such a tax, it is better to err on the low side by permitting only those foreign investments from which the anticipated *after-foreign-tax earnings* exceed the before-tax earnings on home investments. This can be done by disallowing the use of foreign income tax as credit against American tax liabilities. (Note, however, that such a scheme would introduce other market distortions, not affecting the United States, involving the country-location of foreign investments. Since foreign tax rates vary between countries, American investments would be attracted to low-tax countries, rather than to the most profitable locations.) At the same time, foreign profits should be taxed when earned, and not when repatriated to the United

States. Investments in underdeveloped countries can be exempt from the extra tax, giving these countries the benefit of a preferential tax exemption.[16]

A tax of this nature interferes with, but does not displace, the market mechanism, as does the voluntary control program. It would permit the most profitable investments to be made, while restricting the level of capital outflow.

[16]Needless to suggest, a tax system should be based more on neutrality and equity considerations than on balance of payments needs. See L. B. Krause and K. Dam, *Federal Treatment of Foreign Income,* Washington: The Brooklings Institution, 1964.

Part **IV**

Effect of an Atlantic Free Trade
Area on the Domestic Economy

PART IV

Effect of an Atlantic Free Trade Area on the Domestic Economy

In contrast to the effects of the various trade arrangements on the U. S. balance of payments, their direct impact on the domestic economy is likely to be small (see Part I). The differences in that impact between the four alternatives would be even smaller. For that reason it is not useful to examine each of them separately. The AFTA was singled out for close scrutiny, but the techniques followed might also be applied to the other three alternatives.

Chapter 10
Aggregative Effects

A. STATIC WELFARE[1] EFFECTS

Although the estimated increase in U. S. trade is large in comparison with total external trade, it is rather insignificant when compared to the size of the national economy. Gross national product in 1960 was $500 billion. The estimated increase in exports and imports each constitutes less than one-half of 1 percent of GNP. The gain in economic welfare brought about by this increase depends on the extent of resource misallocation it removes.

Conceptually, the imposition of a tariff on a single homogeneous import good, i, involves the economy in both production and consumption costs.[2] Production of i expands, drawing resources away from more efficient uses. The extent of this misallocation depends on the effective tariff rate (although such rates were not used in estimating the changes in trade). On the other hand, consumption of commodity i would decline as its domestic price increases by a fraction of the tariff (or by its full amount), and the consumer is drawn to less desirable substitutes. The extent of this effect depends on the nominal tariff rate. These losses must be balanced against the gain in government revenue, part of which may be paid by the foreign exporters.

[1]The word welfare is used loosely to denote economic efficiency. Distributional effects are ignored.

[2]Note that just like an import duty draws resources from export to import-competing industries, so does an export tax push resources from export to import-competing industries. In both cases the change occurs because the domestic price of exportables declines relative to that of importables as a result of the tax.

120

The incidence of the tariff depends on the relative elasticities of export-supply and import-demand, which thereby determine the effect of the tariff on the terms of trade. The total cost of protection is a composite of these three factors netted against each other. For the country imposing the tariff the cost may be either negative or positive, the latter being the case when the gains from improved terms of trade outweigh the loss from the reduction in the volume of trade. However, for the world as a whole the net effect must be negative, because the gain in the terms of trade of one country is balanced by a comparable loss to the rest of the world, while the loss in the volume of trade is universal and is not balanced by any gain. Our interest is in the effect on the welfare of the United States.

These factors operate in reverse in measuring the welfare gain from trade liberalization. But the extension of this simple model to a multi-product multi-country world involves problems which require drastic simplifications. First, some commodities may cease to be produced altogether as protection is removed; while other products, not presently imported, may begin entering the country. Second, substitutability and complementarity relationships complicate the measurement of the consumer cost of protection, which is conceptually difficult in any case.[3]

The analysis that follows abstracts from these and other complications. For the purpose of simplification it is assumed that AFTA consists of two economies of about equal size, the United States, and all other members combined; and the changes in trade flows resulting from quota liberalization are lumped together with those caused by the removal of the tariff.[4] Figure 1 presents the welfare implications of the increase in imports in partial equilibrium terms. P_F and Q_F are the price and quantity traded, respectively, under free trade. When a tariff is introduced, the export price declines and the import price rises, each by half the tariff (points P_t in quadrants I and III), while the quantity traded declines to Q_t.

Applying the Marshallian concepts of consumers' and producers' surpluses to the increase in imports as the duty is removed, we obtain

[3]For a discussion of these and other problems see Harry G. Johnson, "The Cost of Protection and The Scientific Tariff," *Journal of Political Economy*, August, 1960, pp. 327-45.

[4]The introduction of many countries with less than complete elimination of duties, presents certain complications. See J. E. Meade, *Trade and Welfare*, Oxford University Press, 1955, Chapter 31.

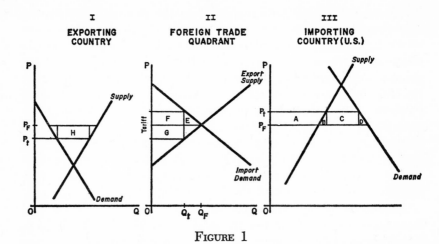

FIGURE 1

the following results: In quadrant III, there is an increase in consumers' surplus represented by the area under the demand curve,
bound by prices P_t and P_F. It is balanced by a loss of producers'
surplus (area A) and government revenue (rectangle C, which equals
rectangle F in quadrant II) The net gain consists of triangles B and D,
which can be referred to as the production and consumption effects,
respectively. They both comprise triangle E in quadrant II. For a
given industry, i, the effect of eliminating this tariff can be measured
by the formula:

$$\frac{1}{4} \cdot \frac{t}{1+t} \cdot d\,P_i + \frac{1}{4} \cdot \frac{t}{1+t} \cdot d\,C_i = \frac{1}{4} \cdot \frac{t}{1+t} \cdot d\,M_i$$

where dP is the reduction in the amount of importables produced,
dC is the increase in the amount consumed, and dM is the increase
in the amount imported. Added over all industries, we get a total of

$$\sum_i \frac{1}{4}\frac{t}{1+t}\,dM_i = \$85 \text{ million.}$$

However, while rectangle C (or F) represents internal redistribution in the importing country from the government to domestic consumers, the government also loses rectangle H in quadrant I (= G
in quadrant II). It represents the part of the duty paid by foreign
exporters, and is equal to:

$$\sum_i \frac{1}{2} M_i \cdot \frac{t}{1+t} = \$385 \text{ million.}$$

(The total loss of government revenue is twice this amount.) For the sake of comparison it might be mentioned that while a free trade area would eliminate government tariff revenue altogether, a reduction in duties may change it in either direction or leave it unaltered, depending on elasticity conditions.

The net welfare effect of the expansion in imports is a loss of $300 million. On the other side of the ledger, American exports are expected to rise by over $2 billion, when the tariff facing U. S. exports is removed. In this case, however, we assume infinitely elastic supply curves in American industries. This implies that resources can be moved easily from the import-competing to the export industries: first, because the quantities involved in such a shift are very small portions of the total resources employed in each industry, and second, because the existence of unemployed resources in the economy helps eliminate "friction." Since the expected increases in imports and exports are roughly equivalent, and abstracting from redistributional effects which might arise from the employment of factors in different proportions in the two kinds of industries, the welfare effect is likely to be nil. There is no producer surplus associated with an infinitely elastic supply curve.

Finally we come to the removal of discrimination against U. S. exports by the European regional groupings raising exports by $450 million. This change can be treated in the same way as the (balanced) increase in exports mentioned in the last paragraph, yielding no welfare gain. But since it is actually an unbalanced change in trade, it is preferable to view it differently. Instead of concentrating on changes in the volume of trade, the focus can be placed on the terms of trade. Thus the discrimination induced loss to nonmember countries can be approximated by estimating the price reductions that would have been necessary to maintain their exports to the EEC and EFTA intact in the face of the discrimination. Assuming away product differentiation, this loss would apply to the entire U. S. sales in the two trade blocs, and removal of the discrimination would result in a corresponding gain. If t is the tariff discrimination in industry i, the gain can be computed according to the following formula:

$$\sum_i \frac{1}{2} \frac{t}{1+t} \cdot E_{U.S.} = \$130 \text{ million}$$

We thus obtain *a net loss (in real terms) to the United States of $170 million*. This result, which might seem peculiar at first sight, is essentially a product of the size of the American economy coupled with the high internal mobility of its resources. The United States can improve its terms of trade at the expense of other nations, through the imposition of a tariff. Elimination of the duty removes this gain. On the other hand, the relative ease with which resources can be transferred (within the relevant range) from one industry to another, precludes any significant loss on the export side when a foreign tariff is imposed. Correspondingly, there would be no gain from the removal of such duty. It should be noted that this estimate is strictly static in nature and is concerned only with reallocation effects. It does not include any losses or gains arising out of dynamic factors. Nor does it include such secondary benefits as the probable reduction in monopoly power within the United States.

B. Effect on Money GNP

The effect of AFTA on money income and output can be divided into three components. First, the increase of the export balance of ($2.488 − 2.183 =) $0.3 billion would have the same multiplied impact as would any rise in spending. Second, the balanced increase in the volume of trade of $2.18 billion *may* have a positive rather than neutral effect on GNP. For while the increase in exports has a full positive (initial) impact on production, the rise in imports may not exert a full negative influence. Instead of displacing fully the consumption of domestically produced goods, part of the increase could be financed by a reduction in consumer savings, when a greater variety of goods becomes available on the domestic market. Consequently, a balanced growth in trade may increase aggregate spending.[5] It is difficult to determine a priori if, and by how much, savings would decline. But since we are dealing mainly in imports which compete directly with close domestic substitutes, it is reasonable to expect a high displacement ratio and a very small increase in total effective demand. For the sake of assumption, we shall tentatively postulate a 5 percent rise in aggregate spending, and show separately the order of magnitude involved. The figure can be disregarded by those who prefer to assume a 100 percent displacement ratio of imports. The third component relates to government policy concerning the $770 million decline in its revenue.

---

[5]See W. Stopler, "The Volume of Trade and the Level of Living," *Quarterly Journal of Economics,* February, 1947.

In order to deal with the first component, we postulate a simplified two-country model: the United States (country a) and the rest of AFTA combined (country b), with 1960 Gross National Product of $500 billions and $390 billions, respectively. The United States is assumed to have a marginal propensity to import (M_a) of 0.05. Since the marginal propensity to import is a product of the average propensity to import and the income elasticity of demand for imports, the assumed M_a is consistent with the average propensity of around 0.04 and income elasticity of about $1\frac{1}{4}$.[6] By contrast, the marginal propensity to import of the rest of AFTA (M_b) is estimated at 0.2.[7] Finally, I shall postulate a marginal propensity to save (s) of 0.3 in both countries.[8] The following estimates are confined to the income effect and abstract from its interaction with prices.

If the autonomous net increases in American exports replaces locally produced products in country b, then the foreign trade multiplier[9] would be:

---

[6]See footnote 41, p. 46, Part II (above) for the import-demand equation. For earlier estimates, see M. E. Kreinin, "United States Imports and Income in the Postwar Period," *The Review of Economics and Statistics*, May, 1960, pp. 223-35.

[7]See J. J. Polak and R. R. Rhomberg, "Economic Instability in an International Setting," *American Economic Review*, May, 1962 (Papers and Proceedings) pp. 110-18.

[8]In dealing with a similar problem, J. Vanek (*International Trade: Theory and Economic Policy* [Homewood, Illinois: R. D. Irwin Inc., 1962], pp. 130-33) postulated a marginal propensity to save of 0.1. This is a reasonable assumption for the relation between private savings and disposable income. But it does not take account of other leakages out of the income stream, such as the one into government tax revenue. Thus, the domestic multiplier, with the government sector, is:
$\dfrac{1}{1-c(1-t)}$ where c is the marginal propensity to consume and t is the marginal tax rate.

[9]See C. Kindleberger, *International Economics* (Homewood: Irwin, 1963), p. 195, and W. R. Allen and C. L. Allen, *Foreign Trade and Finance*, (New York: MacMillan, 1959), p. 263. A general formula, from which both of the above formulas can be derived is:
$$\Delta Y = \frac{A_a\,(s_b + m_b) + A_b \cdot m_b}{(s_a + m_a)\,(s_b + m_b) - m_a m_b}$$
where s and m are respectively the marginal propensities to save and to import, and A represents the autonomous change. In the first case $-A_a = +A_b$ while in the second case $A_b = O$.

$$k = \frac{1}{s_a + m_a + m_b \left(\dfrac{s_a}{s_b} \right)} = 1.8^{10}$$

and the rise in the United States income would be $540 million. On the other hand, if the increase in American exports merely reduces savings in country b, leaving aggregate domestic demand unchanged, the multiplier[11] would be:

$$k = \frac{1 + \dfrac{m_b}{s_b}}{s_a + m_a + m_b \left(\dfrac{s_a}{s_b} \right)} = 3$$

and the increase in U. S. income would be $900 million. Since we are dealing with products in which members of the AFTA compete with each other in the domestic and foreign markets, and under the assumption that all non-U. S. members are one country, the first result is probably closer to reality than the second. It could, however, be supplemented by the effect of the $2.18 billion balanced increase in the volume of trade (second component), resulting in a (2.18 x 5% =) $0.1 billion increase in aggregate demand. The consequent increase in income through the foreign trade multiplier would be $180 million, bringing the total increase to $0.72 billion.

At first sight this increase in money GNP may appear inconsistent with the reduction in real income (arrived at in the last section) coupled with the presumed decline in domestic prices suggested by the removal of the tariff. Actually, however, it is caused by the loss of government revenue to the tune of $0.77 billion, resulting in a comparable budgetary deficit. Any further consequences depend on government policy. If the period under consideration were that of unemployment and excess capacity (removal of tariffs is not likely to take place under such circumstances), the government might wish to leave things as they are. On the other hand, under full employment and unchanged public expenditures the government could decide to recoup part or all of its lost revenue, say, by imposing sales taxes. Depending on the tax multiplier, this would more than offset the gain of $720 million, leading to a net decline in money GNP. Alternatively, the government may wish to adopt a combination of fiscal and monetary

---

[10]This compares to a multiplier of about 1.4 obtained by Polak and Rhomberg (*op. cit.*, p. 114).

[11]See footnote 9 above.

measures, which would exactly neutralize the effect of AFTA on the economy. Assuming no change in government spending, this would involve, first, full restoration of the lost public revenues, by levying $0.77 billion of sales taxes.[12] In addition, the country would lose $170 million worth of real goods (see last section). To match this decline, spending should be lowered by the same amount. And assuming a tax multiplier of around 1½, the government would have to levy $115 million in additional taxes. While neutralizing total expenditures, this policy would result in a government surplus of $115 million, depriving the economy of cash balances. In subsequent years that money would have to be put back into the economy through monetary policy.

C. Effect on Employment

In recent years a considerable amount of information became available on the relationship between foreign trade and domestic employment.[13] None of the studies incorporates the multiplier effect of foreign trade, but most of them include both direct and indirect employment, utilizing input-output tables.

Of the studies listed in the footnote, the most comprehensive one is that of Salant and Vaccara. For each of 72 selected manufacturing industries the authors estimate the following effects of one million dollars increase in imports: a) the direct impact on employment in the selected industry, b) the indirect effect on employment in all other industries traced through interindustry relations data, c) the effect of liberalization on employment in industries connected with

---

[12]The question may be asked: who paid these taxes before? Most directly, the taxes were paid by the importers. Half the total was then shifted to, and paid for by, the American consumer, while the other half was shifted to the foreign producers in the form of lower export prices. Under the assumption of balanced trade accounts before and after AFTA (i.e. no change in reserves), this would have resulted in a reduction of foreign purchases in the United States. Thus, indirectly, the elimination of the $0.77 billion in import taxes led, under our assumptions, to an increase in spending in the domestic economy.

[13]For example, see the following: (1) W. Salant and B. Vaccara, *Import Liberalization and Employment,* Washington, D.C.: The Brookings Institution, 1961. (2) U. S. Department of Labor, Bureau of Labor Statistics (BLS) *Domestic Employment Attributable to U. S. Exports, 1960* and *Employment in Relation to U. S. Imports, 1960* Washington, 1962 (mimeographed). (3) U. S. Department of Labor, BLS, *The Relationship Between Imports and Employment* (an analysis of 27 import-competing industries and 2 industry case studies), Washington, April, 1962 (mimeographed) (4) B. Vaccara, *Employment Implication of Trade with the Common Market,* September, 1962 (mimeographed).

the process of importation such as ocean freight and insurance, and d) the direct and indirect effect of higher foreign incomes and dollar earnings on American exports and employment. Items (a) and (b) are usually negative,[14] while (c) and (d) are positive. The four components are then combined to obtain the net short-run employment effect of trade liberalization in each industry. Of the 72 industries, the net decrease in employment is largest for the liberalization of apparel products where it is 175 employees, and smallest for grain mill products where there is a net increase of five. A summary of the main findings (as given in Table 10.1, p. 215 of their book) is reproduced in Table 13.

Table 13

Employment Effects of Import Liberalization in 72 Industries

(Number of employees per million dollars increase in imports)

	First Quartile	Median	Third Quartile
(1) Gross Decrease (Direct and Indirect)	94	115	135
(2) Gross Increase Associated with Shipping of Imports	0	1	2
(3) Gross Increase Associated with Exports	19	26	50
(4) Net Decrease	57	86	104

These figures must be regarded as *upper limits* for two reasons. First, some of the assumptions made, like that of "equivalent displacement" of domestic production by imports, may result in an overstatement of the employment effect of trade liberalization. Second, the authors' attempt to examine the current validity of the estimates, which are based on 1953 data, leads them to conclude that "in most cases studied, liberalization undertaken in 1960 would cause smaller . . . effects on employment . . . than is indicated by the estimates of this study" (p. 236).

If we accept the figure of 114 as the average decline in employment resulting from one million dollars increase in imports (the direct and indirect effects minus employment associated with the process of importation), and apply it to the expected $2.18 billion increase in imports[15] as a result of the AFTA, we obtain a decline in employment

---

[14]In many cases (a) and (b) were found to be of roughly equal size.

[15]The change in landed and f.o.b. prices would be about the same. To convert f.o.b. to landed price we must add the cost of ocean transportation, insurance, etc. On the other hand, the customs duties collected on all imports must be subtracted.

of 249 thousand workers. Likewise Salant and Vaccara (Table 5.1, p. 113) estimate the median increase in employment per one million dollars increase in exports in each of the 72 selected industries at 107. The $2.49 billion expected increase in exports would result in a gain of 266 thousand jobs. Roughly speaking, the AFTA would cause a net gain of 17 thousand jobs.

For several reasons the Salant-Vaccara estimates are not suitable for the purpose at hand. First they relate to the early 1950's while our trade figures are those of 1960. Second, the 72 selected industries may not fully represent all the products covered by AFTA; on the other hand they include several food items which are not included in this study. Third, their estimates are based on the industry distribution of actual foreign trade, which may not correspond to that of the estimated changes in trade.

As an alternative, we examined the BLS 1960 employment estimates. In *Employment in Relation to U. S. Imports,* all 1960 imports ($14.7 billion f.o.b. and $17.6 billion c.i.f., of which $17.1 billion were considered in the study), were divided into two categories: supporting imports, which account for 60 percent ($10.3 billion) of the total, and competitive imports, comprising 40 percent of all imports ($6.8 billion). All manufactured imports (divisions 19-39) fall into the second category, and indeed account for most of it ($6.3 billion).

Two aggregate estimates were then constructed. The first shows that 941.2 thousand workers were involved in import-related activities.[16] Most of these jobs evidently concern the processing of nonindustrial products, and are not relevant for our purposes. The only pertinent figure is the number of jobs created by the importation process of industrial products (e.g., shipping, insurance, etc.). This was estimated by Salant and Vaccara to average (median) one job per million dollars of imports.

The second estimate relates strictly to the $6.8 billion competitive

---

[16]This estimate includes employment in: (1) the transporting, handling, and distributing of imports from the foreign ports through the U. S. ports to domestic factories that process imported raw materials and to wholesalers that import and distribute finished manufactures; (2) supplying fuel and supplies to the trade and transportation sectors; (3) processing imported raw materials and semimanufactures; and (4) replacing plant and equipment used up in these stages of handling imports. The processing estimate is limited to direct employment in the first-stage processing of imports considered primarily "supporting." It does not include the additional indirect employment involved in providing materials, supplies, and services for the processing of these imported materials.

imports, and shows the number of workers that would have been required to produce them in the United States. It consists of: (a) direct employment, (b) indirect employment, and (c) employment required to replace plant and equipment consumed in these stages of handling. For estimating the indirect employment, the 1947 input-output table was used, updated whenever necessary to reflect 1951-53 relationships. In total, the BLS estimates that 916.2 thousand workers would be required, directly and indirectly, to produce all the competitive imports, 73.7 thousand would be needed to replace the plant and equipment consumed, and 83 thousand workers would be necessary to handle transportation and distribution to the next stage of marketing. The total is 1,072.9 thousand workers, yielding an average of $\left(\frac{1,072,900}{6,808.6} = \right)$ 157.6 workers[17] per million dollars worth of competitive imports. The average for direct and indirect labor is 135, and for direct labor alone—64 workers per $1 million of imports. The arithmetic average of 135 derived here is higher by 20 workers than the median of 115 presented by Salant and Vaccara for "gross decrease." But the two estimates relate to different universes, since the BLS study includes non-manufactured products while the Salant-Vaccara study is confined to selected manufacturing industries.

On the export side, the BLS pamphlet *Domestic Employment Attributable to Exports, 1960,* shows that 3,081,700 workers were required to produce $22,055.3 million worth of exports. These figures average out to 138.7 workers per $1 million of exports.

Although these data are very useful for policy purposes they cannot be directly applied to the estimation of the effect of AFTA on employment, since they relate to all trade, including trade in agricultural products. The two pamphlets present the direct and indirect effect *on* each two-digit industry; they do not show the employment consequences of output changes *in* each industry. While for the direct impact the two figures are identical, the indirect effect caused by each industry is not given, and we cannot estimate it. Consequently, it is not possible to separate out the sectors which do not concern us.

A 1960 employment matrix, prepared by the Bureau of Labor Statistics,[18] was used to overcome this deficiency. For each of some

---

[17]This is the arithmetic average, not a median.

[18]I am grateful to Dr. Jack Alterman of the BLS for making the matrix available.

200 industries in the economy, the table shows the number of jobs required, directly and indirectly, to produce $1 million of output in 1960. The indirect requirements are further subdivided into six major sectors (agriculture, mining, manufacturing, transport, trade, and all others), but they contain no estimate for the replacement of capital goods. In order to use these estimates, the changes in trade caused by AFTA in the 85 SITC groups had to be allocated to the four- and five-digit SIC categories. However, since such a conversion is beyond the means of an individual investigator, we allocated (with the aid of intermediate conversion to Schedules A and B in some cases) the prospective changes in trade among the two-digit SIC industries.[19] By the same token, the BLS employment estimates were collapsed, by the use of arithmetic averages, into the two-digit SIC divisions.

Table 14 presents estimates of the employment changes in each industry (last two columns), obtained by applying the BLS coefficients (first column) to the estimated changes in trade under AFTA. Total gain in employment resulting from the expansion of exports is 247.1 thousands jobs, with three industry divisions: chemicals, nonelectrical machinery, and transportation equipment accounting for over one-half of the total. The employment loss caused by the expansion of imports would be 231.2 thousand jobs, with textile mill products, apparel, and miscellaneous products accounting for over a third of the total. Both the gain and the loss are about equally divided between direct and indirect effects. On balance, the table shows a net gain of 16 thousand jobs as a result of AFTA. Detailed distribution of the indirect effects are given in Appendix Tables IV-A, B, C.

Several adjustments must be made in the aggregate estimates. First, the increase in imports would require on the average (according to Salant and Vaccara) an additional worker per $1 million for handling the merchandise, yielding a gain of 2.2 thousands jobs. Second, allowance must be made for employment attributable to the replacement of plant and equipment consumed. The figures provided in the BLS pamphlets (*op. cit.*) relate to total (including agriculture) exports and competitive imports; and show 9.5 and 10.8 workers, respectively, per $1 million of trade. From them we obtain a gain of 23.6 thousand jobs and a loss of 23.6 thousand jobs attributable to plant

---

[19]Over 10 percent of the total trade was not assigned to individual industries. For these products, the overall mean job requirement (105.2 workers per $1 million of final demand) was used.

Table 14

Employment Effects of Trade Liberalization (SIC Industries)
(1960 Jobs)

SIC No.	Industry Description	Job requirements per $1m of final demand	Changes in Trade ($ millions)		Changes in Employment (Jobs)	
			Imports	Exports	Imports	Exports
22	Textile Mill Products	144.75	196.2	55.4	28,399.95	8,019.15
23	Apparel and Related Products	178.18	165.7	24.1	29,524.43	4,294.14
24	Lumber and Wood Products	114.32	27.1	3.3	3,098.07	377.26
25	Furniture and Fixtures	117.86	10.0	3.5	1,178.60	412.51
26	Paper and Allied Products	68.29	165.9	53.3	11,329.31	3,639.86
27	Printing and Publishing Products	94.96	13.0	15.1	1,234.48	1,433.90
28	Chemicals and Allied Products	111.06	85.2	368.9	9,462.31	40,970.03
29	Petroleum Products	71.67	0	30.1	0	2,157.27
30	Rubber and Plastic Products n.e.c.	88.61	62.2	37.4	5,511.54	3,314.01
31	Leather and Leather Products	114.54	43.9	7.2	5,028.31	824.69
32	Stone, Clay, and Glass Products	87.55	129.6	35.3	11,346.48	3,090.51
33	Primary Metal Products	78.19	171.8	174.5	13,433.04	13,644.15
34	Fabricated Metal Products n.e.c.	97.41	107.4	99.4	10,461.83	9,682.55
35	Machinery, Except Electrical	92.93	101.9	504.7	9,469.57	46,901.77
36	Electrical Machinery	94.30	147.0	157.2	13,935.60	14,823.96
37	Transportation Equipment	98.65	175.3	419.9	17,293.34	41,423.13
38	Instruments and Related Products	102.77	121.2	131.7	12,455.72	13,534.81
39	Miscellaneous Manufactured Prod.[1]	103.49	198.2	77.1	20,511.72	7,979.08
19	Ordnance and Accessories		9.3	1.1⎱		
99	Other		1.0	1.2⎰	1,053.66	227.26
	Not Assigned (Use Arith. Average)	105.2	252.0	289.0	26,510.40	30,402.80
	Total		2,183.0	2,488.0	231,252.26	247,152.90

1. In computing this industry, MM162 (cork products) was excluded because it requires an unusually large number of indirect jobs, but is hardly represented in the trade figures.

SOURCE: See text.

and equipment consumed. Inclusion of these adjustments yields a net gain of 18 thousand jobs. This figure should be at least doubled to allow for the multiplier effect. But it would also be affected by possible government action with respect to the lost public revenue. In any event, the change is rather insignificant compared to a total labor force of over 70 million or even to the 16.7 millions employed in the manufacturing sector of the economy.

The small net gain in employment can be regarded as the result of two conflicting forces. On one hand there is the favorable effect of the $0.3 billion increase in the trade balance. Had the average labor input coefficient of 105.2 jobs per $1 million of output been used throughout, the resulting gain in employment would have been around 31.5 thousand. This figure corresponds to the effect of AFTA on money GNP, and can be further adjusted to allow for a multiplier effect and possible government action, in a manner outlined in section B. On the other hand, the expansion of exports tends to be concentrated in industries with lower labor coefficients than the industries experiencing the increase in imports. This reflects the redistribution of income away from labor and in favor of capital, and reduces the gain in employment by 14.5 thousand.

All the figures presented in this chapter must be regarded as rough orders of magnitude. Yet, despite the high margin of error attached to them, they do point to one important conclusion: Even complete elimination of trade barriers on industrial products would have a relatively insignificant impact on the domestic economy. However, individual trade-oriented industries may be strongly affected.

Chapter 11
Disaggregative Effects

Because of data constraints, this final section will be limited to manufactured products, namely sections 5-8 SITC, exclusive of the unwrought metals. The disaggregative approach employed in Part II makes it possible to identify the individual industries which are likely to sustain a net loss or gain in the event of AFTA. By subtracting for each three- or five-digit SITC group, the anticipated rise in imports from the expected increase in exports, we arrive at a list of industries in which the net change exceeds $50 million (Table 15).

Major gains are concentrated in the various machinery groups (division 7 SITC) and certain chemical specialties. These are also the industries which would derive the main benefit from the elimination of the EEC and AFTA discrimination. On the other hand, large potential losses are registered in manufactured products classified chiefly by materials (division 6), clothing, footwear, and watches and clocks.

As might be recalled, the lists were derived by applying fairly uniform elasticities to the tariff rates and to the 1960 trade figures. The appropriateness of this approach as being too "mechanistic" was questioned at that point, and the relationship of the figures to comparative advantage considerations was discussed on a priori grounds. Table 15 sheds additional light on this relationship. The main losers tend to be labor intensive industries in which the United States (as the relatively capital abundant country) has a comparative disadvantage. On the other hand, the main gainers can generally be classi-

Table 15

Major SITC Industries Affected by AFTA

SITC Number	Description	ΔX-ΔM After Tariff Elimination	ΔX From Removal of European Discrimination	Balassa Index
	Main Gainers			
599	Misc. Chemical Material and Products	65	43	200
714	Office Machinery	42	13	157
715	Metalworking Machinery	71	28	173
716, other than 08	Conveying, Hoisting, Excavating, etc. and Industrial Machinery	235	70	143
732 other than 01 & 03	Other Road Motor Vehicles	96	36	164
734	Aircraft	129	47	331
	Main Losers			
641	Paper and Paperboard	−129		76
653	Other Textile Fabrics Standard Type	− 87		40
666	Pottery	− 47		3
699	Manufactures of Metals, n.e.s.	− 66		81
732-01	Passenger Road Motor Vehicles Complete	− 58		29
841	Clothes Except Fur Clothing	−121		29
851	Footwear	− 65		7
864	Watches and Clocks	− 63		23
899	Manufactured Articles, n.e.s.	− 58		151

SOURCE: See text.

fied as capital intensive, in which the United States enjoys a comparative advantage.

Perhaps more significant is the relationship of the results to the index of "revealed" comparative advantage developed by Balassa in an attempt to determine the list of industries in which each industrial country enjoys comparative advantage.[20] The index is based on relative export shares for the main industrial nations, where the expression "relative share" refers to the ratio of the percentage share of Country E exports of commodity j in world exports of the same commodity to the total share of Country E in world exports of manufactured goods.[21] Because it requires only data on international trade,

---

[20]See B. Balassa, "Trade Liberalization and 'Revealed' Comparative Advantage," *The Manchester School*, May, 1965, pp. 99-123.

[21]By "world exports" is meant the exports of the ten major industrial countries.

the index can be computed for the comparable commodity groups in the SITC.

The index is developed as follows: First, two formulas are computed to show the relative share of Country E exports of commodity j in the first and second periods (average for the years 1953-1955 and 1960-1962, respectively):

$$(1)\ \frac{E_{j0}}{T_{j0}} \bigg/ \frac{E_{t0}}{T_{t0}} \qquad\qquad (2)\ \frac{E_{j1}}{T_{j1}} \bigg/ \frac{E_{t1}}{T_{t1}}$$

where E and T relate to the export of the country in question and to world export respectively; subscripts j and t refer to commodity j and to all manufactured goods, and subscripts 0 and 1 denote the two time periods considered. Then the relative share in the second period is shown as a percentage of that in the first (base) period, so as to impart a dynamic element to the concept:

$$(3)\ \frac{\dfrac{E_{j1}}{T_{j1}} \bigg/ \dfrac{E_{t1}}{T_{t1}}}{\dfrac{E_{j0}}{T_{j0}} \bigg/ \dfrac{E_{t0}}{T_{t0}}}$$

Finally, the index of "revealed" comparative advantage is expressed as the arithmetic average of equations (2) and (3). This expression reflects the assumption that past trends can be expected to continue, at a declining rate as compared to the past.

The results for the industries concerned are reproduced in the last column of Table 15. As expected, the "gainers" register above 100 on the index, while the prospective losers are well below 100. The only major exception is industry 899—manufactured articles not elsewhere specified. This is a catch-all item in the trade statistics, and the figures included in it probably suffer most from too high a level of aggregation. Needless to suggest, even this index cannot account for unforeseen future developments. For example, the American competitive position in the aircraft industry (the strongest shown on the Balassa index) may or may not weaken in the future, depending in part on the outcome of the U. S.-European competition in the development of the supersonic transport.

In order to examine more closely the domestic implications of the trade changes, it is necessary to convert the SITC groups that exhibited major changes to their four- and five-digit SIC components. However, since it is not possible to undertake such a conversion (except on a high level of aggregation, which is unlikely to reveal any significant effects) a reversed (improvised) method was used in order to identify two groups of industries: the export group which stands to derive considerable benefit from AFTA; and the import-competing group, which would lose by the creation of AFTA. We first selected detailed SIC groups that are heavily involved in foreign trade, and then checked the probable effect of AFTA by placing them in the SITC groups to which they belonged. Following are the criteria used in the selection:

Export Industries:

(a) Four- or five-digit SIC industries that export at least $50 million, and whose exports constituted at least 5 percent of shipments in three out of the five years (1958-1962). *Or:*

(b) Industries that export at least 10 percent of shipment, and whose exports exceed $10 million in three out of five years. *And:*

(c) SIC industries so selected must belong to an SITC group where the expected net increase in export to AFTA is at least $30 million or more.

Import-competing Industries:

(a) Four- or five-digit SIC industries that import at least $25 million, and whose imports constitute at least 5 percent of new supply in three out of five years (1958-1962). *Or:*

(b) Industries that import at least 10 percent of new supply, and whose imports exceed $10 million in three out of five years. *Or:*

(c) For very heavily protected industries[22] (where low imports might have been caused by a high level of protection), imports must be at least $5 million and 3 percent of new supplies in three out of five years. *And:*

(d) SIC industries so selected must belong to an SITC group where the expected increase in imports from AFTA amounts to $20 million or more.

Tables 16 and 17 present the two lists of industries selected under the above criteria. In addition, there would be indirectly affected industries; namely, industries heavily involved in supplying those listed in the tables. I attempted to identify them by using the 1958 O.B.E.

---

[22]Industries classified as class 4-b in Appendix Table 7 of B. N. Vaccara, *Employment and Output in Protected Manufacturing Industries,* Washington: The Brookings Institution, 1960.

Table 16

SIC Export Industries Expected to Benefit (Directly) from AFTA (Shipments, Exports, and Export-Shipment Ratio)

SIC Code	Description of Industry	Shipments ($ millions)		Exports ($ millions)		Exports as a Percentage of Shipments	
		1960	1962	1960	1962	1960	1962
2221, 2262	Man-made and silk broad-woven fabrics	1,384.7	1,559.7	85.5	84.6	6	5
2815	Intermediate and tar products, dyes, pigments	1,012.6	1,049.5	81.3	86.4	8	8
2818	Industrial organic chemicals n.e.c.	3,116.3	3,453.8	189.2	192.9	6	5
2861	Gum and wood chemicals	182.6	180.8	62.2	41.7	34	23
28730, 28790, 28184	Agricultural insecticide chemicals and formulations	507.4	626.8	90.2	119.1	18	19
28993, 28185, 28198, 9 2899	Misc. chemical preparations, n.e.c.	1,650.3	1,785.0	293.8	331.2	18	19
34431, 3	Heat exchangers and steam condensers; steel power boilers and parts	442.9	463.6	49.2	132.8	11	29
3511, 3519	Steam engines, turbines, turbo-generators, and parts; Internal combustion engines, n.e.c.	1,837.9	1,866.4	220.0	248.6	12	15
3531, 2	Construction and mining machinery and equipment			789.9	839.2	33	35
3533	Oil field machinery and equipment	506.6	551.4	159.6	142.9	32	26
3537	Industrial trucks and tractors	389.5	394.4	40.7	40.1	10	10
3541	Metal cutting machine tools and parts	746.8	831.2	127.8	205.1	17	25
3542, 35485	Machine tools, metal-forming, and parts	400.5	417.3	88.8	124.0	22	30
35481-4	Metal working machinery, except machine tools	582.3	610.5	130.5	157.2	22	26
3584, 3551-5, 8	Machinery and parts for food products, textiles, wood-working, pulp and paper industry, printing trades and special industry	2,770.2	3,028.7	497.8	596.6	18	20
3561	Pumps and compressors	1,106.7	1,147.3	142.2	157.0	13	14
3562	Ball and roller bearings and parts	836.2	937.9	55.7	62.2	7	7
3567	Industrial furnaces and ovens and parts	214.6	194.2	23.1	32.9	11	17
3569	General Industry machinery and equipment, n.e.c.	246.8	608.0	23.1	72.2	9	12
3571	Computing and related machines	1,279.2	1,637.5	169.7	270.6	13	17
3585, 35811	Refrigerators and refrigeration machinery, except household	1,683.1	1,852.7	145.8	155.0	9	9
3717 (2, 3)	Trucks and motor coaches	2,742.6	3,087.9	382.1	253.7	14	9
372	Aircraft and parts	11,488.5	11,999.9	1,759.0	1,987.4	15	17

SOURCE: See text and Table 17.

Inter-industry Relations study.[23] But that study is too aggregative for the purpose at hand, with the manufacturing sector broken into 52 two- or three-digit SIC industry groups.

Table 17

SIC Import-Competing Industries Expected to be Injured by AFTA
(Shipments, Imports, and Import-New Supply Ratio)

SIC Code	Description of Industry	Shipments ($ million)		Imports ($ million)		Imports as a Percentage of New Supply	
		1960	1962	1960	1962	1960	1962
2231	Wool, broadwoven fabrics and blankets	677.7	690.3	80.5	75.9	11	10
2271, 2	Carpets and rugs, woven and tufted	770.1	925.3	49.2	48.0	6	5
2279	Carpets, rugs, and mats, n.e.c.	53.7	44.2	5.8	4.8	10	10
22992	Textile goods, n.e.c.	49.2	45.3	135.4	181.1	73	80
2381, 2259	Dress and work gloves, except leather	147.1	176.6	22.6	23.6	13	12
26211	Newsprint	248.9	265.6	688.7	695.8	73	72
2815	Intermediate coal tar products, dyes, pigments	1,012.6	1,049.5	27.8	41.9	3	4
3151	Leather gloves	55.1	45.2	12.6	25.3	19	36
3211, 32313	Flat glass	754.8	679.7	50.8	51.7	6	7
3262	Vitreous china table kitchenware	49.0	47.8	23.4	24.8	32	34
3263	Earthenware food utensils	62.2	50.2	13.0	13.6	17	21
33152	Steel nails and spikes	132.7	138.7	39.0	40.0	23	22
33312, 33412, 33512	Refined copper and alloys copper alloys-rolled, drawn, etc.	1,783.1	2,045.6	180.7	122.2	10	6
3421	Cutlery	177.1	207.4	10.2	11.6	6	5
3871	Watches and clocks	386.7	405.1	62.6	67.7	14	14
3872	Watch cases	28.1	25.6	5.3	5.6	16	18
3913	Lapidary work	46.0	48.5	91.6	103.4	67	68
3914	Silverware and plated ware	203.6	215.4	29.9	27.7	13	11
3941	Games and toys, n.e.c.	568.5	690.5	34.7	41.4	6	6
3942	Dolls	198.3	200.9	9.1	20.0	4	9
3949	Sporting and athletic goods, n.e.c.	661.9	654.9	26.8	34.7	4	5
3961, 39112	Jewelry (including costume), except platinum and carat gold	311.4	318.3	28.6	33.1	8	9
3962	Feather, plumes, and artificial flowers	60.2	55.1	39.5	43.8	40	44
3963	Buttons	73.5	76.8	6.8	6.5	6	8
3995	Umbrellas, parasols, and canes	33.9	34.1	3.9	5.7	10	14

SOURCE: Bureau of Census, *U. S. Commodity Exports and Imports as Related to Output,* 1962 and 1961, 1961 and 1960.

---

[23]See M. Goldman, M. Martimont and B. Vaccara, "The Interindustry Structure of the United States—A Report on the 1958 Input-Output Study," *Survey of Current Business,* November 1964, pp. 10-29. The study was prepared by the Office of Business Economics (O.B.E.).

The same shortcoming applies to the input-output employment data provided by Salant and Vaccara for 72 industries[24] (relating to 1952-53). Although in many industries, the indirect effects of import liberalization exceed half the total effects, they are spread over several industries. Therefore, in any one case, only rarely does one industry suffer (or enjoy) a concentrated indirect impact. On the other hand, an industry can appear as an indirect loser (or beneficiary) several times (namely, as a result of trade expansion in several industries), and the total may be of significant proportions. Unfortunately, the estimates given are too aggregative. Inasmuch as each of the 72 industries contain several (or many) four- and five-digit SIC groups, the total indirect effects shown would be considerably understated. Furthermore, these effects are only broken into 40 groups, of which only 24 are in the manufacturing sector.

Bearing in mind these limitations, I have tentatively concluded from the 1958 O.B.E. study that "primary iron and steel manufacturing" (SIC 331, 332, 3391, 3399) would be a major indirect gainer, while the "fabrics, yarn and thread mill" industry (SIC 221-224, 226, 228) would be a main indirect loser.

As a final step, the Census of Manufactures was used to identify the geographical regions in the United States that may be strongly affected by AFTA.[25] Considering only the direct effects, and allowing for some aggregation dictated by the availability of data, it appears that the East North Central[26] and Pacific[27] regions stand to gain the most from the expansion of exports. In terms of both employment and value added, there is an above average concentration of those industries included in Table 16 in these two regions. On the other hand, New England,[28] and the Mountain [29] states would suffer most from the establishment of AFTA.

---

[24]W. Salant and B. Vaccara, *Import Liberalization and Employment,* Washington, The Brookings Institution, 1961, Appendix Tables F-1 and F-2.

[25]For a study of the geographical origin of American exports in 1960, see Bureau of the Census, *Current Industrial Reports,* series M.161(60)-1, released on May 4, 1960.

[26]Includes the states of Ohio, Indiana, Illinois, Michigan, and Wisconsin.

[27]Includes the states of Washington, Oregon, California, Alaska, and Hawaii.

[28]Includes the states of Maine, New Hampshire, Vermont, Massachusetts, Rhode Island, and Connecticut.

[29]Includes the states of Montana, Idaho, Wyoming, Colorado, New Mexico, Arizona, Utah, and Nevada.

Appendix Table IV-A

Job Requirements Per $1 Million of Final Demand in 1960

SIC Division	Total Employment	Direct Employment	Indirect Employment	Indirect Employment Breakdown					
				Agriculture	Mining	Manufact.	Transport.	Trade	All Other
22	144.75	62.89	81.86	49.99	1.28	15.14	5.29	6.25	3.91
23	178.18	79.08	99.10	37.51	1.29	42.95	4.39	8.23	4.73
24	114.32	75.45	38.87	5.12	1.02	21.85	5.49	2.15	3.24
25	117.86	58.85	49.01	5.41	1.22	32.56	4.06	2.98	2.78
26	68.29	36.98	31.31	1.55	2.05	15.53	6.78	3.10	2.30
27	94.96	71.73	23.23	.87	.80	13.07	3.30	1.96	3.23
28	111.06	32.81	78.25	30.44	4.02	26.21	7.92	4.83	4.83
30	88.61	47.31	41.30	9.00	2.04	21.45	3.43	3.01	2.37
31	114.54	82.03	32.51	4.06	.73	19.38	3.17	2.73	2.44
32	87.55	59.96	27.59	1.00	4.82	12.00	5.74	1.48	2.55
33	78.19	44.92	33.27	.31	8.17	14.88	4.86	2.85	2.20
34	97.41	53.77	43.64	.40	2.18	32.68	3.67	2.65	2.06
35	92.93	55.53	37.40	.38	1.37	29.15	2.58	2.16	1.76
36	94.80	55.47	39.33	.74	2.04	28.49	2.96	2.84	2.26
37	98.65	43.86	54.79	1.27	1.97	41.47	4.47	3.13	2.48
38	102.77	65.61	37.16	2.63	1.17	24.70	2.66	3.52	2.48
39[a]	103.49	66.30	37.19	2.88	1.41	24.25	2.82	3.25	2.58
Average (Arith.)	105.20	58.97	46.23	9.03	2.21	24.46	4.33	3.36	2.84

a. In computing this industry, MM 162 (Cork products) was excluded because it requires an unusually large number of indirect jobs, but is hardly represented in the trade figures.

SOURCE: Derived from the 1960 BLS Employment Matrix.

Appendix Table IV-B

Employment Effects of the Changes in Export Under AFTA (1960 Jobs)

SIC Division	Total Employment	Direct Employment	Indirect Employment	Indirect Employment Breakdown					
				Agriculture	Mining	Manufact.	Transport.	Trade	All Other
22	8,019.15	3,484.11	4,535.04	2,769.44	70.91	838.76	293.07	346.25	216.61
23	4,294.14	1,905.83	2,388.31	903.99	31.09	1,035.09	105.80	198.34	113.99
24	377.26	248.98	128.27	16.90	3.37	72.10	18.12	7.09	27.19
25	412.51	240.97	171.53	18.93	4.27	113.96	14.21	10.43	9.73
26	3,639.86	1,971.03	1,668.82	82.61	109.26	827.75	361.37	165.23	122.59
27	1,433.90	1,083.12	350.77	13.13	12.08	197.35	49.83	29.59	48.77
28	40,970.03	12,103.61	28,866.42	11,229.32	1,482.98	9,668.87	2,921.69	1,781.79	1,781.79
29	2,157.27	NA	NA	NA	NA	NA	NA	NA	NA
30	3,314.01	1,769.39	1,544.62	336.60	76.30	802.23	128.28	112.57	88.64
31	824.69	590.62	234.07	29.23	5.26	139.54	22.82	19.66	17.57
32	3,090.51	2,116.59	973.93	35.30	170.15	423.60	202.62	52.24	90.01
33	13,644.15	7,838.54	5,805.61	54.09	1,425.66	2,596.56	848.07	497.32	383.90
34	9,682.55	5,344.74	4,337.82	39.77	216.70	3,248.39	364.80	263.41	204.76
35	46,901.77	28,025.99	18,875.78	191.79	691.44	14,712.00	1,302.13	1,090.15	888.27
36	14,873.96	8,719.88	6,182.68	116.33	320.69	4,476.63	465.31	446.45	355.27
37	41,423.13	18,416.81	23,006.32	533.27	827.20	17,413.25	1,876.95	1,314.29	1,041.35
38	13,534.81	8,640.84	4,893.97	346.37	154.09	3,252.99	350.32	463.58	326.62
39	7,979.08	5,111.73	2,867.35	222.05	108.71	1,869.67	217.42	250.57	198.92
19+99	199.88	112.04	87.84	17.16	4.20	46.47	8.23	6.38	5.40
Not Ass.	30,402.80	17,042.33	13,360.47	2,609.67	638.69	7,068.94	1,251.37	971.04	820.76
Totals	247,152.90	124,767.15	119,983.62	19,565.95	6,353.05	68,804.15	10,802.41	8,026.38	6,386.87

SOURCE: See Table IV-A and text.

Appendix Table IV-C

Employment Effects of Changes in Imports Under AFTA (1960 Jobs)

SIC Division	Total Employment	Direct Employment	Indirect Employment	Indirect Employment Breakdown					
				Agriculture	Mining	Manufact.	Transport.	Trade	All Other
22	28,399.95	12,339.02	16,060.93	9,808.04	251.14	2,970.47	1,037.90	1,226.25	767.14
23	29,524.43	13,103.55	16,420.87	6,215.41	213.75	7,116.81	727.42	1,363.71	783.77
24	3,098.07	2,044.69	1,053.38	138.75	27.64	592.13	148.78	58.27	87.80
25	1,178.60	688.50	490.10	54.10	12.20	325.60	40.60	29.80	27.80
26	11,329.31	6,134.98	5,194.33	757.14	340.10	2,576.43	1,124.80	514.29	381.57
27	1,234.48	932.49	301.99	11.31	10.40	169.91	42.90	25.48	41.99
28	9,462.81	2,795.91	6,666.90	2,593.49	342.50	2,233.09	674.78	411.52	411.52
30	5,511.54	2,942.68	7,568.86	559.80	126.89	1,334.19	213.35	187.72	147.41
31	5,028.31	3,601.12	1,427.19	178.23	32.05	850.78	139.16	119.84	107.11
32	11,346.48	7,770.82	3,575.66	129.60	624.67	1,555.20	743.90	191.80	330.48
33	13,433.04	7,717.26	5,715.79	53.26	1,403.61	2,556.38	834.95	489.63	377.96
34	10,461.84	5,774.90	4,686.94	42.96	234.13	3,509.83	394.16	284.61	221.24
35	9,469.57	5,658.51	3,811.06	38.72	139.60	2,970.38	262.90	220.10	179.34
36	13,935.60	8,154.09	5,781.51	108.78	299.88	4,188.03	435.12	417.48	332.22
37	17,293.35	7,688.66	9,604.69	222.63	345.34	7,769.69	783.59	548.69	434.74
38	12,455.72	7,951.93	4,503.79	318.76	141.80	2,993.64	322.39	426.62	300.58
39	20,511.72	13,140.66	7,371.06	570.82	279.46	4,806.35	558.92	644.15	511.36
19+99	1,073.04	601.49	471.55	92.11	22.54	249.49	44.17	34.27	28.97
Not Ass.	26,510.40	14,860.44	11,649.96	2,275.56	556.92	6,163.92	1,091.16	846.72	715.68
Totals	231,252.26	123,901.70	107,356.56	23,669.47	5,404.62	54,432.32	9,620.95	8,040.45	6,188.68

SOURCE: See Table IV-A and text.

Index

Ad valorem rates, 15, 32-37, 53, 56

AFTA. *See* Atlantic Free Trade Area

Aircraft, 56, 62, 138

Atlantic Free Trade Area:
  aggregate effects on U. S. economy:
    employment, 129-33
    exports and imports, 138-39; *see also* Exports; Imports
    gross national product, 124-127
    static welfare, 120-24
  alternative policies, 69-79
  basic tenet of, 90
  comparison of effects on U. S. external trade under, and under alternatives, *Table,* 74
  disaggregative effects, 134-40
  East North Central (U. S.) gains under, 140
  effect on exports, 134-38:
    discrimination, 58-64
    estimated increase, 56-57
    import demand elasticity, 54-56
    nonagricultural materials, 58
    prices, 54
    quotas, 57
    tariff rates, 53-54
  effect on imports, 134-39:
    elasticity, 40-47
    estimated increase, 47-48
    industrial materials, 50-52
    nonindustrial commodities, 50-52
    prices, 38-40
    quotas, 49-50
    tariff, 31-37
      83-84, 85:
    balance of payments, 101-05

  effect on U. S. foreign investments, costs and marketing, 86-88, 89, 92
    questionnaire on, 106-09; analysis of, 90-100
    U. S.: reactions of U. S. firms, 90-100; real income and, 110-15; reduction or consolidation of foreign operations under, 93-94; trade, effect on, 65-68
  expansion of foreign operations under, 96-99
  Great Britain warned against, 25 n. 36
  implications of, 29
  industries affected by (increase or injury), 15, 56, 134-37; *Tables,* 30, 48, 65, 135, 138, 139
  percentage import-export trade, 29-30
  political considerations, 23-26
  pressures on EEC to join, 71 n. 77
  regional gains or losses under, 140
  tariff rates, 31-37
  trade figures published, 29-30

Agriculture:
  complementary commodities, 6
  employment study in, 131
  European domestic policies, 70
  foreign investments, 86, 103, 104
  importance of exports to, 6-10, 12; *Tables,* 7, 8
  perishable products, 92
  protectionism, 23, 25, 26.
  See also Foodstuffs

Alternative policies, 69-79; *Table,* 74

American Management Association Seminar, 54

144

plants in, *Table*, 103; value of direct foreign investments in, *Table*, 83

Low tariff club, 25

Manufactured products, defined, 7, 29

Manufacturing and industry:
  balance of trade and, 49-50, 102, 109-14
  closed economy, 5
  discrimination, *Tables*, 62, 63
  duty free imports, 31-32
  effects of trade liberalization on, *Table*, 132
  employment studies, 130-31
  European aversion to U. S. control, 89
  European investments in U. S., 83-84
  exports: industrial, 62-63, 71; total in 1960, 29-30; under AFTA, EEC, EFTA, 71-72; U. S. leading, 5
  exports and imports, relation to domestic production and consumption, *Table*, 8
  extractive industries, labor costs in foreign investment, 87
  finished products, percentage of all exports, 7
  gross national product, 5, 7
  foreign trade, 7-10, *Table*, 7
  imports: total under AFTA, 71; total in 1960, 29-30, 71
  in middle to high tariff bracket, 32
  independence from foreign trade, 59
  industries: abrasives, 98; air conditioning and refrigeration, 96; coal, 26, 50, 59; container and packaging, 98; conveying, hoisting, excavating, etc. machines, 56, 132; diesel engines (French), 57; elastic fibers, 95, 96; electrical, 48, 56, 63, 93, 94, 97, 99, 130; engine bearings, 98; equipment manufacturing, 98; fiber containers, 99; floor covering accessories and supplies, 98; footwear, 48, 134, 135; heating, plumbing, air conditioning, 92; household appliances, 95; hydraulic cylinders, 94; industrial and automotive belts, 95; industrial machinery (various), 29, 56, 62, 63, 92, 94, 95, 131, 132, 134, 135;

industrial equipment and electronic components, 98; iron and steel (*See* Iron and steel industry); instruments and related products, 132; lead, 17 n. 24, 50, 51; leather and leather products, 132; lubricants and related materials, 50; lumber and wood products, 132; metals, 48, 98, 132, 135; mining and smelting, 102, 104, 131, 138; nonferrous metals, 17 n. 24, 30 n. 2; office furniture, 98, 99; ordnance and accessories, 132; paper and paper board, 48, 135; paper and allied products, 132; pens, 94; petroleum, 25, 26, 50, 51, 102, 132; pharmaceutical products, 99; piping systems, 93; pottery, 135; printing and publishing products, 132; records, 95; road motor vehicles, 56, 62, 63, 135; rubber and plastic products, 132; semimanufactures, 51; semiprocessed goods, 86, 103; shipping, 129; stone, clay and glass products, 132; supersonic transport, 136; trade industry, 131; transport, 131; transportation equipment, 131, 132; typesetting machines, 97; unwrought nonferrous metals, 50, 134; valves, 94; vehicles, 48; watches and clocks, 48, 134, 136; zinc, 17 n. 24, 50, 51; *See also Tables*, 138, 139

labor intensive industries, 134

quotas, 65

resource oriented industries, 92

tariff, 65

U. S. European investments, 83-84

See also Elasticities; Employment; Exports; Foodstuffs; Foreign investments; Foreign trade; Gross national product; Imports; Iron and steel industry; N o n a g r i c u l t u r a l commodities

Marketing, 88

Marshall Plan, 3, 119

Matrix, on 1960 employment, 129, 130-31

MFN. *See* Most favored nation

Military considerations, 11-26

dissertation on two-digit commodity
groups, 78 n. 82
major industries and AFTA, 134-35,
Table, 135
SIC-SITC conversion study, 29 n. 1
Static welfare, 120-24
Steel. *See* Iron and steel industry
Survey of Current Business, 83
Sweden, 12, 23 n. 32, 34
Switzerland, 12, 71 n. 77, 93
Subpoena power, 17-18

Tariff,
ad valorem equivalents, 15, 32-37,
53, 56
attitude of economist toward, 13-14
capital movements, 90-100
comparative advantage, 40-41
comparison: Europe-U. S., 35
coverage, 31-32
conversion, 32-37
effects of AFTA, 120-33, 134-40
effects on: balance of trade, 29-52;
domestic economy, 118-24; industries, 9. *See also* Manufacturing
and Industry; processing and fabri-
cating of goods, 32
elasticity. *See* Elasticity
escape clause, 13, 14, 16-20, 18,
19 n. 29, 21, 42
external, 70
factor proportion theory, 41
formula estimating increased U. S.
imports under AFTA, 47-48
higher rate on manufactured goods,
34
in alternative policies, and AFTA,
29-37
index of protection (Vaccara), 32, 41
items taxed 41 percent or more, 35
lowered in Germany and Western
Europe, 54-55
mechanistic approach, 41-42
on industrial products, 23, 25, 26
policies affecting foreign investments,
88
political aspects, 11-13
raise in, 18, 45
rates, 53-54
reductions, 13-20, 22, 34, 40-47
removal, 38-40

restrictions, 29, 66
trade liberalization and, 90-100
unimportance of in AFTA, 92.
See also Exports; Imports
Taiwan, 49
Taxes, sales, 127 n. 12
Technological progress, effect on economy, 6 n. 6, 17 n. 23, 67
Textiles, 48-50, 94, 132, 135, 138
Trade adjustment assistance, 20-21
Trade Agreements Act of 1934:
discrimination, 59
explanation of, 13-26
escape clause, 13, 14, 16-20, 21
extension during 1950's, 15
Extension Act (1958), 15-20
national security provisions, 13, 18,
52
peril point, 16-19, 21, 42
presidential power in, 18, 21, 22
subpoena power, 17-18
trade adjustment assistance, 20-21
Trade Expansion Act of 1962, 12, 22-23,
52
Trade not aid policy, 14
Transportation costs, 86-87, 88, 92, 93,
95, 98
Tropical goods, 6, 22, 86
Turkey, 54, 57

Umbrella price argument, 38
Underdeveloped countries, 5 n. 5, 73-74
United Kingdom:
Common Market and, 70
domestic demand elasticity, 43
effect of customs union, 69 n. 75
entry into EEC advocated by U. S.,
12
industrial commodities discrimination, 63
not EEC member, 71 n. 77
ratio of consumption, 55, 56
tariff rates, 34, 35, 54
U. S.: direct foreign investments in,
83; food plants in, 93;
warned against AFTA, 23 n. 36
United Nations:
Commodity Trade Statistics, 77
Monthly Bulletin of Statistics, 77

Index of Names

153

PUBLICATIONS OF THE DIVISION OF RESEARCH

BUREAU OF BUSINESS AND ECONCMIC RESEARCH

MSU BUSINESS STUDIES

ELECTRONICS IN BUSINESS
Gardner M. Jones
Stanley C. Hollander

ELEMENTARY MATHEMATICS OF LINEAR
PROGRAMMING AND GAME THEORY
Edward G. Bennion

EXPLORATIONS IN RETAILING
MARGINAL ASPECTS OF MANAGEMENT PRACTICES
Frederic N. Firestone

HISTORY OF PUBLIC ACCOUNTING IN THE UNITED STATES
James Don Edwards

CONTRIBUTIONS OF FOUR ACCOUNTING PIONEERS
James Don Edwards
Roland F. Salmonson

LIFE INSURANCE COMPANIES IN THE CAPITAL MARKET
Andrew F. Brimmer

BUSINESS CONSULTANTS AND CLIENTS
Stanley C. Hollander

THE AUTOMOTIVE CAREER OF RANSOM E. OLDS
Glenn A. Niemeyer

ELECTRONIC COMPUTATION OF HUMAN DIETS
Victor E. Smith

INTERNATIONAL ENTERPRISE IN A DEVELOPING ECONOMY
Claude McMillan, Jr., Richard F. Gonzalez
with Leo G. Erickson

THE ENTERPRISING MAN
Orvis F. Collins, David G. Moore
with Darab B. Unwalla

AGRICULTURAL MARKET ANALYSIS
Vernon L. Sorenson, editor

LABOR MARKET INSTITUTIONS AND WAGES IN THE
LODGING INDUSTRY
John P. Henderson

THE EXECUTIVE IN CRISIS
Eugene Emerson Jennings

BANKING STRUCTURE IN MICHIGAN: 1945-1963
Robert F. Lanzillotti

RETAIL DECENTRALIZATION
Eli P. Cox and Leo G. Erickson

BANK ADMINISTERED POOLED EQUITY FUNDS FOR
EMPLOYEE BENEFIT PLANS
Frank L. Voorheis

THE PERFORMANCE POST AUDIT IN STATE GOVERNMENT
Lennis M. Knighton

INSTITUTE FOR INTERNATIONAL BUSINESS AND ECONOMIC
DEVELOPMENT STUDIES

MSU International Business and Economic Studies

MICHIGAN'S COMMERCE AND COMMERCIAL POLICY STUDY
John L. Hazard

INTERNATIONAL DIMENSIONS IN BUSINESS
Recent Readings from BUSINESS TOPICS

MANAGEMENT DEVELOPMENT AND EDUCATION IN
THE SOVIET UNION
Barry M. Richman

THE UNITED STATES OVERSEAS EXECUTIVE: HIS
ORIENTATIONS AND CAREER PATTERNS
Richard F. Gonzalez and Anant R. Negandhi

STEEL AND ECONOMIC DEVELOPMENT: CAPITAL
OUTPUT IN THREE LATIN AMERICAN STEEL PLANTS
David G. Greene

ALTERNATIVE COMMERCIAL POLICIES—
THEIR EFFECT ON THE AMERICAN ECONOMY
Mordechai E. Kreinin